WALKING IN KENT

About the Author

Kev Reynolds is a freelance writer, photojournalist and lecturer whose first title for Cicerone Press (*Walks & Climbs in the Pyrenees*) appeared in 1978, and is still in print. He has also published a number of trekkers' guides to Nepal and, nearer to home, several guides on walking in southern England. As well as compiling guidebooks, he writes regular features for the outdoor press, produces brochures for tourist authorities, and leads trekking holidays in various high mountain regions. The first honorary member of the British Association of European Mountain Leaders (BAEML), and a member of the Alpine Club, Austrian Alpine Club and Outdoor Writers' Guild, Kev's enthusiasm for the countryside in general, and mountains in particular, remains undiminished after a lifetime's activity. When not trekking or climbing in one of the world's great ranges, he lives among what he calls 'the Kentish Alps', and during the winter months regularly travels throughout Britain to convey that enthusiasm through his lectures. Check him out on www.kevreynolds.co.uk

Cicerone titles by the same author

Alpine Points of View
Walks & Climbs in the Pyrenees
Walking in the Alps
The Pyrenees
100 Hut Walks in the Alps
The Wealdway & Vanguard Way
Walks in the Engadine
Walking in Kent Vols I & II
Walking in the Valais
Walking in Sussex
The Bernese Alps
The South Downs Way
Ticino – Switzerland
The North Downs Way
Central Switzerland

The Cotswold Way
The Jura (with R. Brian Evans)
Annapurna – a Trekker's Guide
Tour of the Jungfrau Region
Everest – a Trekker's Guide
Alpine Pass Route
Manaslu – a Trekker's Guide
Chamonix to Zermatt – the
    Walker's Haute Route
Kangchenjunga – a Trekker's Guide
Langtang, Helambu & Gosainkind
    – a Trekker's Guide
Tour of Mont Blanc
Tour of the Vanoise
Écrins National Park

WALKING IN KENT

by

Kev Reynolds

CICERONE

2 POLICE SQUARE, MILNTHORPE, CUMBRIA LA7 7PY
www.cicerone.co.uk

© Kev Reynolds 2007
ISBN 13: 978 1 85284 462 2   1852844620

A catalogue record for this book is available from the British Library.
Photographs by the author

Dedication

This book is for Billy Moon, in the hope that he too will be inspired, uplifted and enriched by the natural world that is his inheritance.

Acknowledgements

Wandering through this county of ours, I am acutely aware of the gratitude we owe to many farmers, landowners, private individuals and members of various rambling clubs, who undertake work to improve the quality of our footpaths, help maintain the numerous stiles and gates, or who are vigilant in regard to problems of access. I am thankful, too, to the county's Rights of Way officers and their staff for ensuring that our footpaths are, on the whole, in pretty good condition and reasonably well waymarked. Once again I am indebted to Jonathan Williams at Cicerone for agreeing to yet another book of Kent walks, and to his team for putting it together. Joining me on some of these walks – and in so doing adding to their enjoyment – were my daughter Claudia, her partner Kelvin, and our good friend Chitra, while my wife shared the joy of plotting the walks in advance on our well-used maps, and then walked every route with me in all seasons and in all weathers. Once again, this book is as much hers as it is mine.

Advice to Readers

Readers are advised that while every effort is taken by the author to ensure the accuracy of this guidebook, changes can occur which may affect the contents. It is advisable to check locally on transport, accommodation, shops, etc., but even rights of way can be altered. Paths can be affected by forestry work, landslip or changes of ownership.

The author would welcome information on any updates and changes sent through the publishers.

Front cover: Orchards above Yalding – the 'garden of England' (Walk 18)

CONTENTS

PREFACE

As I write a great spotted woodpecker hangs from the bird feeder outside my window, its crimson under-belly and extravagantly blotched wings destroying any hope of camouflage. For long moments it seems nervously alert, head cocked this way and that, red eye blazing. Then it bursts into action with a sudden sharp prod of its long beak, followed by a brief pause. Then another prod, and another and another and another in quick succession, while blue tits and great tits wait impatiently for their turn in a disorderly queue on the camellia bush. Meanwhile, the robin – always one for the main chance – knows it has no opportunity to get at the feeder, so takes its place directly beneath, hoping for something to fall.

Another movement catches my attention, and a dormouse, whose nest is in the retaining wall that supports the vegetable garden, dashes across the weather-stained rocks and disappears from view. What is he hoping for? I wonder.

Sometimes a cock pheasant trespasses into the garden. On occasion a pair have been seen perched side-by-side on the fence, gazing over the meadow next door like two dreamy pensioners watching the tide come in.

Beyond the fence that meadow folds gently down to woodland. In it three ponds attract activity. Canada geese have recently taken an interest in the largest

The oasts of Outridge Farm are an eye-catching feature at French Street (Walk 3)

of these. Mallard were there first, but coot and moorhen have long been established in the two nearest to our cottage. One day last summer I had to wade into one of those ponds to rescue a ewe that'd fallen in and was about to drown. It's out there now with its week-old twin lambs. Black faces and black socks, the lambs are already joining others that race around the meadow with the boundless energy and uncontrolled excitement we witness among their sort every spring.

I feel it too.

The countryside explodes with goodness. All the energy stored through the long months of winter is being set free. You can sense it with the first hint of dawn when birds begin their anthems to the new day. It's there through the lengthening hours of sunlight and showers, and continues to percolate while evening slides towards nightfall.

This is no time to be at the word processor!

Most days before resuming work after lunch, I wander onto the crown of the hill just a few short minutes away. I don't know how many hundreds of times I've been up there in the past 30-odd years – in all weathers, in all seasons, at all times of day and night. But the magic never dims. There's an immense view, you see, that reaches into three counties. The land falls away to the south, east and west, spreading out in a patchwork of green and blue; the green of field and meadow, the blue of woodland and a line of hills that rims a far horizon.

Apple blossom underlines Kent's claim to be the Garden of England

Octavia Hill, one of the co-founders of the National Trust and a passionate advocate of the countryside, loved this place, and she must have had it in mind when she wrote of 'the healing gift of space'. That's precisely what I experience when out walking. The healing gift of space.

Fortunately, Kent has a lot of it – a lot of space from which to experience that healing gift. This book explores some of the best.

From the North Downs to Romney Marsh, from the Greensand Hills to the orchards and hop gardens of the Weald, and from the Medway's banks to the White Cliffs of Dover, Kent has a remarkably diverse set of landscapes. Within them tiny villages, remote churches, isolated farms, manor houses and bow-walled cottages all resonate with history, and are linked by footpaths that are our oldest highways.

Highways? Kent has more miles of motorway than any other county. Speeding across the county, they give a false impression. The beauty of Kent and its seemingly endless acres of green are barely glimpsed by the motorist, and those who stick to the roads will never appreciate just how much open, uninhabited space there is; how much natural beauty lies waiting to be explored. 'They only know a country who are acquainted with its footpaths,' wrote Richard Jefferies more than a hundred years ago. 'By the roads, indeed, the outside may be seen; but the footpaths go through the heart of the land.'

It's true. The only way to properly explore this, or any other county, is by shunning mechanised transport in favour of walking.

Walking, after all, brings an intimate relationship with the land, for you move at just the right pace to capture and absorb its very essence; its basic structure, its clothing of vegetation, its watercourses, its wide range of habitats and inhabitants. Motoring shields you from reality. Walking puts you in touch with every nuance of the season; for if you are observant you will not only *see* the land in a visual sense, but taste it, smell it, hear its breath, feel its goodness; become *aware* of its very nature.

Walking in Kent gives unbounded opportunities to do just that.

Research for this third collection of Kent walks has provided the best of all excuses to explore and observe the county's wonderland of space (as if an excuse were needed). Through a lively correspondence readers of the previous two volumes have been asking for more. After giving a lecture recently on *The Best of Kent*, which reveals the county from a walker's viewpoint, a lady handed me her much-used copy of Volume I. Grubby from use and minus its cover, it was held together with rubber bands. 'I think it's time we had a new edition,' she said. 'Don't you?'

Resembling a water-tower, Little Chart church beckons across the fields (Walk 22)

Well, this is it. It includes a few favourites from Volumes I and II, all rewalked and largely rewritten, to bring them up-to-date. But it also includes many new routes whose discovery served as yet another reminder of what a delightful county this really is. Though my work among mountains takes me to some of the world's most dramatically spectacular places, there is nowhere I'd rather live than here, and every day spent walking the footpaths of Kent has served only to deepen my love for this place.

So, if this collection of walks brings you as much pleasure as my wife and I harvested whilst working them out, it will have served its purpose. But I'm painfully aware that the countryside is constantly evolving, that agriculture is once again at a crossroads, and the whole question of land management is under review. Bearing these things in mind, changes are almost inevitable within the print run of this book. Changes to field and woodland boundaries, the grubbing out or enlargement of orchards, vineyards or hop gardens; the surfacing of a farm track perhaps, or diversion of a footpath around a new building. All or any of these things may affect the accuracy of some of my route descriptions; in which case I offer my apologies in advance, and ask for your understanding.

Should you find that a section of a walk described within these pages is no longer valid, I'd appreciate a note giving specific details, and I'll check it out in advance of any future edition. Correspondence may be addressed to me c/o Cicerone Press, 2 Police Square, Milnthorpe, Cumbria LA7 7PY.

My thanks in advance. May you enjoy each day as the adventure it is.

Kev Reynolds
Easter, 2006

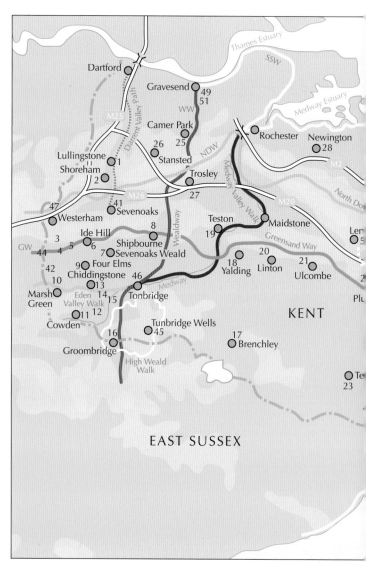

Location of Walks

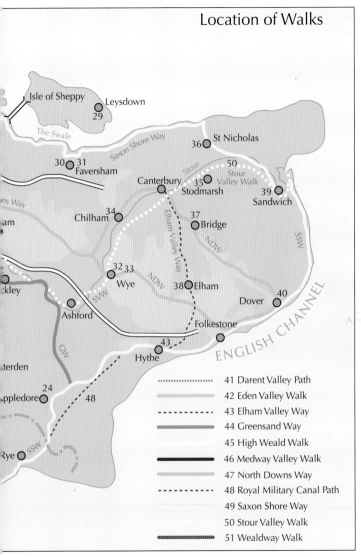

Isle of Sheppy Leysdown
29

The Swale

Saxon Shore Way

36 St Nicholas

30 31 Faversham
Faversham

Canterbury 35 50
Stour Valley Walk
Stodmarsh

39
Sandwich

Chilham 34

37 Bridge

32 33
Wye

38 Elham

Dover 40

Ashford

Folkestone

43
Hythe

ENGLISH CHANNEL

24
Appledore

48

Rye

SSW

.... 41 Darent Valley Path
———————— 42 Eden Valley Walk
– – – – – – – 43 Elham Valley Way
———————— 44 Greensand Way
45 High Weald Walk
———————— 46 Medway Valley Walk
47 North Downs Way
- - - - - - - 48 Royal Military Canal Path
49 Saxon Shore Way
50 Stour Valley Walk
———————— 51 Wealdway Walk

On the way to Egerton, the North Downs are seen in the distance (Walk 22)

INTRODUCTION

KENT – A WALKER'S COUNTY

The diverse nature of its landforms makes Kent a wonderland to explore on foot, and with more than 4200 miles (6876km) of footpaths, bridleways and byways criss-crossing the county, the walker is spoilt for choice. Every natural feature has its own particular charm, and every season its own brand of beauty.

The chalk ridge of the **North Downs** stretches right across the county in an extensive arc reaching from Westerham to Dover. Covering almost a quarter of the county, the Kent Downs region was designated an Area of Outstanding Natural Beauty in 1968. Though one side of the ridge slopes gently to the Thames and Medway estuaries, or off to the Swale or low-lying Thanet, its 'front' makes an abrupt, steeply pitched wall that acts as a natural boundary to the Weald. Far-reaching vistas from the scarp edge provide a bonus to explorations, while secluded hamlets nestle in folds of the back-country to underline their apparent isolation. The chalk being overlaid in places with clay and flint makes this a fertile land, and in both the back-country and on the broad downland crest, large arable fields and sheep-grazed meadows act as springboards from which larks rise singing. Step lightly as you explore, for deer may be seen straying from cover; there are fox-runs and badger trails, and wild flowers that adorn meadow and woodland alike – especially the orchids and cowslips that are so characteristic of the Downs.

For the long-distance walker, the North Downs Way keeps mostly to the scarp edge on its 130-mile (208km) journey from Farnham in Surrey to Dover, with an alternative section that breaks away near Wye to visit Canterbury before curving round to the coast. The Pilgrims Way, however, traces a route along the base of the Downs, but as this is tarmac road for most of the way, it's lost much of its appeal for walkers. Not so the broad crest, the scarp edge and the inner valleys where abundant opportunities exist for walks of varying lengths; delightful half-day rambles or full-day walks, some of which can be found in this book – from Lullingstone, Shoreham, Camer Country Park, Stansted and Trosley and Wye.

The **Greensand Hills** act as an inner lining to the North Downs. But the ridge which shadows that downland

Bluebell woods add colour to Mariners Hill (Walk 5)

wall is much narrower and more clearly defined than its better-known neighbour, and the views arguably even better from its crest. Overlooking the Weald, this ridge also stretches right across the county, entering Kent from Surrey a little south of Westerham, and making a long curve towards Hythe and the edge of Romney Marsh. Unlike the chalk Downs, the Greensand Hills are, as their name suggests, sandy in places – although this is not evident everywhere. The vegetation is different, with bracken-covered heaths, stands of pine and birch and many handsome beechwoods. The hurricane winds of October 1987 flattened vast areas of woodland, but time has served to heal the landscape and, following programmes of replanting, large wooded sections have recovered well. One of the legacies of that hurricane is the welcome spread of bluebells, wood anemones and wood sorrel, so walking along the Greensand Hills in springtime can be truly spectacular.

While the North Downs wall is accompanied for much of its length by major roads, the ridge of Greensand has been spared such company, and rewards with some of the finest, and most extensive uncluttered views, not only in Kent, but in all of southern England. With so many great vantage points to exploit, walks along the Greensand Hills count among the best of all. Westerham, Crockham Hill, Toys Hill, Ide Hill, Sevenoaks Weald, Shipbourne; all these give memorable days out. But so do Yalding and Linton, where the south-facing slopes are hung with orchards; and Ulcombe and Pluckley from whose footpaths you gaze across great open spaces. For the long-distance walker the Greensand Way traces a route along the ridge for 110 miles (177km) between Haslemere in Surrey and Hamstreet, south of Ashford, and is a very fine route indeed. Recognising this, a few sections of that long trail are adopted by circular walks described in this book.

In common with the North Downs and Greensand Hills, **The Weald** is not confined to Kent, but spreads beyond the county's boundary into Surrey and Sussex. This vast region is contained by the North and South Downs and consists of a complex series of fertile hills and vales, among which are to be found the fields of soft fruit, the platts of cobnuts, the orchards, vineyards and hop farms that gave Kent the epithet the 'Garden of England'. But there are also large areas of meadowland and extensive woods; and in Wealden hollows hammer ponds, now a haven of peace and tranquillity, recall a time when they were at the heart of England's 'black country' as local iron ore was smelted then hammered into cannon. Centuries later heron stalk the margins of these ponds, whose outlet streams flow between banks bright with wild flowers. Fine houses built by the iron masters remain largely tucked away, but some are seen from walks included here. Elsewhere, several of Kent's loveliest villages punctuate the Wealden landscape, their sturdy churches beckoning across the acres, their streets lined with black-and-white half-timbered houses and pubs.

Groombridge Place has a moat around it (Walk 16)

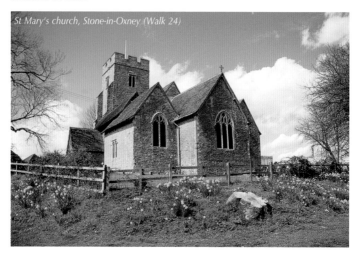

St Mary's church, Stone-in-Oxney (Walk 24)

The Wealdway makes a roughly north–south crossing of 82 miles (131km) from Gravesend on the Thames to Beachy Head and Eastbourne in Sussex; and the High Weald Walk follows nearly 28 miles (45km) of footpaths on a circuit near Tunbridge Wells. However, within this collection of walks, those that begin in the far west of the county at Four Elms, Marsh Green, Cowden, Chiddingstone, Penshurst and Groombridge are full of variety, while routes that explore the Weald's rolling hills around Brenchley and Tenterden are no less rewarding.

Kent's long **Coastline** is forever changing. While the tides chew away at the coastal fringe in some places, in others land is reclaimed from the sea. Nothing illustrates this changing

shape of the county more vividly than a walk along the Saxon Shore Way, from Gravesend to Hastings in Sussex. When the Romans arrived here they found a very different coastline from that which we would recognise today, for although some of it has disappeared beneath the waves, elsewhere we now walk on one-time sea-cliffs several miles inland!

Separating the Isle of Sheppey from mainland Kent, the Swale is edged on both shores with mudflat and marshland loud with wildfowl, while the River Wantsum (which until the Middle Ages was as wide as the Swale and, linked with the Stour, helped make Thanet an island) is now a minor stream, beside which ploughs turn the soil where ships once sailed. The White Cliffs of Dover remain white because they're crumbling;

were they not they'd be green like the band of grassed-over cliffs at Stone-in-Oxney. Stone, of course, is now marooned from the sea by the expanse of Romney Marsh, but look at the map and allow imagination to roll back the centuries, and you'll see how things once were. Some of the walks in this book can bring history alive if you understand the clues, and those that follow the coastline as it is now – near Leysdown on Sheppey, for example, or routes near Newington, Faversham, Sandwich and Dover – illustrate the diverse nature of coastal scenery. The walk on Chislet Marshes from St Nicholas at Wade, and that which includes Appledore and Stone-in-Oxney, take footpaths where a few centuries ago it would have been necessary to travel by boat.

Of Kent's **Rivers**, the Medway is perhaps the best known. Dividing the county in two, it was once renowned for separating Kentish Men from the Men of Kent – the former were born west of the river, with Men of Kent to the east – but few bother with that distinction today. Rising among the hills of Sussex, the Medway draws from many sources, and by the time it reaches Tonbridge is substantial enough to be navigable by barge. Plans to extend the navigation as far as Penshurst failed, yet today there are no less than 10 navigational locks and flood control sluices between Leigh and Allington. A towpath accompanies the river from Tonbridge to Maidstone, giving a delightful 16-mile (25km) walk. A continuation as far as Rochester (not

The Medway below East Farleigh (Walk 19)

towpath but on paths that are either on the riverbank or not far from it) adds another 12 miles (19km) to what is known as the Medway Valley Walk. In this present collection of walks, that which starts from Teston Bridge enjoys one of the best sections along the Medway's valley.

While the Medway divides the county into west and east, that other long river, the Stour, makes a writhing journey from its source near Lenham to the sea at Pegwell Bay, via Ashford, Canterbury and Sandwich. This too is a delightful river, but its character is quite different from that of the Medway's. Meandering through downland, woodland, orchards and hop gardens, it almost loses its identity on entering Canterbury. But that identity is regained outside the city walls, and just beyond Fordwich (which lays claim to being Britain's smallest town) it snakes among lakes, dykes, and a magical marshland nature reserve. One walk suggested from Stodmarsh unravels some of the mystery of this utterly charming district, while the Stour Valley Walk journeys for a little over 51 miles (82km) from source to sea. The Stour and the Medway are both rivers of character, but the little Nailbourne stream is sometimes dry for months – or even years – at a time. However, the valley it drains is a delight of small villages linked by the 22.5 miles (36km) of the Elham Valley Way, sampled here on walks from Bridge and Elham itself.

NOTES FOR WALKERS

Walking is a year-round activity, and need not be confined to the dry summer months, for there is as much beauty to be found in the countryside in the leafless months of winter as in vibrant spring and the golden days of autumn. As long as you're properly attired, the weather is rarely so extreme as to keep the true country lover indoors, and some of our most enjoyable days spent researching the walks for this book took place in frost, wind and rain.

Choose clothing and footwear suitable for the season, bearing in mind the changeable nature of Britain's weather. No specialised equipment will be required for tackling these walks, but comfortable footwear is important. While shorts may be suitable for summer walking on most of these routes, do bear in mind that brambles and nettles often stray across infrequently used paths. Carry a pair of overtrousers (preferably with a generous zipped ankle-gusset to enable you to pull them on and off without first removing boots) to protect your legs from the discomfort of walking through high or wet vegetation. Whether trekking in the Alps, high Himalaya or the Kent countryside, I recommend a lightweight, collapsible umbrella for those times when you're caught out by the rain. Not only will it keep you dry, it can help protect the top of your rucksack from getting wet, and will be indispensable for walkers who wear glasses.

Most of the county's footpaths are well signed and waymarked

It's worth carrying a few plasters in case of blisters, or the odd scratch or two, and whether or not you plan to buy refreshment should a pub or café be on the route, I'd advise taking a flask of drink and a few nibbles in case your energy wanes.

An Ordnance Survey map will be needed in the unlikely event of your becoming lost, and it will also give a broader picture of the countryside you're walking through than will be gained from the OS extracts provided within these pages. Details of specific sheets required are given at the head of each walk description. A note of refreshment facilities to be found en route is also given. Most of these will be at country pubs, although I'm at pains to stress that I have no personal experience of any of those mentioned, so no endorsement of services provided is intended. (Truth is, I'd rather lounge beneath a tree with a view and chew on an apple, than sit in a pub with a pint and a snack.) But should you plan to call at a wayside pub or café, please be considerate if your footwear is wet or muddy, and either remove your boots or cover them with plastic bags.

One would assume that anyone choosing to go for a walk would be a lover of the countryside and treat it with respect. Sadly, litter can still be found in places where only the walker is likely to go. It is not only unsightly, but can cause injury to wildlife and farm animals. So please be scrupulous and leave no litter, but instead help make the countryside even more attractive by removing any rubbish you find. A plastic bag is useful for packing it away. Maybe then walkers will put to shame those few farmers who discard fertiliser bags that become snagged in hedgerow and ditch, or who leave items of once-expensive machinery to rust in a field.

Please remember that most footpaths cross private land – be that farmland or historic estate. But a public right of way is just that; it forms part of the Queen's highway and is subject to the same protection in law as other highways. However, footpaths may not always be clearly evident on the ground, in which case I trust directions in this guidebook will enable you to follow the correct route without difficulty. Where paths lead through growing crops, please walk in single file to avoid damaging that crop or trespassing. Treat fields of grass as you would those of ripening wheat, and always use stiles or gates where provided to cross hedges, walls and fences, and after use refasten any gates found closed.

Take extra care when crossing or walking along country lanes. Keep to the right-hand side to face oncoming traffic, and walk in single file. Use a grass verge wherever possible.

Crops and animals are a farmer's livelihood and should be left undisturbed. Sheep and cattle will be found grazing on a number of these walks, so please keep dogs under control at all times. Farmers have a right to shoot any dogs found worrying livestock.

For the purposes of this book, Kent has been divided into two sections – **West Kent and the Weald**, and **North and East Kent** – with the M20 corridor effectively carrying the line of division (see the 'Location of Walks' map).

Maps

Within the main body of this guide, sections of the Ordnance Survey map relevant to each walk described are taken from the 1:50,000 series (1¼in = 1 mile), which should be adequate to provide an overview of the route. However, greater detail and a wider perspective may be gained from consultation with the Explorer series of maps published at a scale of 1:25,000 (2½in = 1 mile). The recommended sheet for each walk is noted in the panel at the head of that walk's description.

Grid references are frequently quoted to enable you to locate a given position on the OS map, each sheet of which is divided into a series of vertical and horizontal lines to create a grid (the British National Grid). Each of these lines is given a number which is quoted at the top, bottom and sides of the sheet, with numbers increasing from left to right for the vertical lines (known as 'eastings'), and from bottom to top for horizontal lines ('northings').

Route symbols on OS maps

~~~ route

~~ alternative route

◀ route direction

🚶 start point

🚶 finish point

🚶 start/finish point

For OS symbols key see OS maps

To identify an exact point on the map from a given grid reference, take the first two digits from the six-figure number quoted. These refer to the 'eastings' line on the OS map. The third digit is estimated in tenths of the square when moving to the right from that line. Next, take the fourth and fifth digits referring to the 'northings' line, and then the final digit estimating the number of tenths of the square reading up the sheet.

Times and Distances

Distances quoted in the text, although taken directly from the OS map, are approximations only, but should be reasonably accurate. Please note that heights quoted on OS maps are given in metres, rather than in feet, and that grid lines are spaced 1km apart. The text in this book, however, gives both imperial and metric measurements.

Reckon on walking about 2–2½ miles (3–4km) per hour, without prolonged stops, but bear in mind that your pace will be slower after wet

23

weather when conditions may be heavy under foot. Allow extra time when accompanied by children or inexperienced walkers – or, indeed, when walking in a group.

Kent County Council has produced a pack of route descriptions for eight walks having wheelchair access: *Walks for All in Kent & Medway*. At the time of writing these can also be downloaded from the website **www.kent.gov.uk/countrysideaccess**

Public Transport and Car Parking
It is not practical to give details of all bus and train services in Kent, since they may change within the period this guidebook is in print. However, an indication of some routes is provided in the information panel at the head of specific walk details.

For rail information, including times and fares, either enquire at your local railway station, telephone National Rail Enquiries on 08457 484950, or look on the internet – **www.nationalrail.co.uk**

For bus services, call Travel-line 0870 608 2608.

If you must use your own transport and are in doubt how to find the start of a walk by road, download a free road map via **www.streetmap.co.uk** and type in the name of the town or village where the walk begins. Then click 'search'. A detailed map of the district will appear, and this can be printed off.

At the head of each walk description in this book, the location and grid reference of a parking facility (where known) is given. However, where there is no official parking area, please park sensibly and with consideration for local residents, and leave access for farm vehicles and so on. If parking near a church, please avoid service times. Do not leave any valuables in your vehicle, and be sure to lock your car before setting out on your walk.

The Royal Military Canal was intended to hold back Napoleon's army (Walks 24 & 48)

The Country Code

- Enjoy the countryside and respect its life and work
- Guard against all risk of fire
- Fasten all gates
- Keep dogs under close control
- Keep to public paths across farmland
- Use gates and stiles to cross fences, hedges and walls
- Leave livestock, crops and machinery alone
- Take litter home
- Help to keep all water clean
- Protect wildlife, plants and trees
- Take special care on country roads
- Make no unnecessary noise

It was Octavia Hill, that indomitable Victorian champion of the countryside and co-founder of the National Trust, whose prescient words sum up the spirit of the Country Code:

Let the grass growing for hay be respected, let the primrose roots be left in their loveliness in the hedges, the birds unmolested and the gates shut. If those who frequented country places would consider those who live there, they would better deserve, and more often retain, the rights and privileges they enjoy.

As winter gives way to spring countless banks turn yellow with primroses

WEST KENT AND THE WEALD

From the Darent Valley which slices through the North Downs, to the low-lying pastures edging Romney Marsh, the countryside south of the M20 rewards the walker with a magnificently diverse set of landscapes. Only a small part of the North Downs is included, but the Kentish half of the Greensand Ridge is here in its entirety, as is the vast sweep of the Weald with its historic villages, orchards, hop gardens and vineyards, and numerous scenes of timeless beauty.

Shoreham, a neat village in the Darent Valley (Walk 7)

WALK 1
Lullingstone Park – Shoreham – Lullingstone Park

Distance	6.5 miles/10.5km
Maps	OS Explorer 147 'Sevenoaks & Tonbridge' and 162 'Dartford' 1:25,000
Start	Lullingstone Park Visitor Centre (grid ref 526638)
Access	Via Castle Road cutting southwest off A225 0.5 mile/800m south of Eynsford railway bridge
	Nearest railway station: Eynsford
Parking	At the Visitor Centre
Refreshments	Cafeteria at Lullingstone Park Visitor Centre; pubs in Shoreham

Formerly a medieval deer park, Lullingstone Park provides a focus of outdoor recreation on the west flank of the Darent Valley between Shoreham and Eynsford. In addition to the ubiquitous golf course, there are woodland walks and views from open meadows, while the Visitor Centre on the Darent's bank serves the public with refreshments, toilet facilities, interpretive leaflets, walking guides and plenty of information on the area's natural history.

Apart from the pleasures of the North Downs, there are many other features to this walk. First, a riverside stroll with views across a man-made lake to the Tudor manor house of Lullingstone Castle, then an opportunity to make a short diversion to inspect the remains of a Roman villa. There are handsome farmhouses and flint-walled cottages, an imposing mansion set in neat lawns, and a rather striking viaduct marching across the valley. Near the end of the walk, Shoreham has lots of interest and attractive scenes at almost every turn.

From the Visitor Centre entrance take the very pleasant streamside path among trees, with the Darent on your right. Beyond the stream can be seen an extensive lake that extends as far as the red-brick mansion of

The Queen Anne façade of Lullingstone Castle conceals a Tudor mansion

Lullingstone Castle. Walk through a parking area and onto a lane by the Castle's gatehouse entrance. Keep on this lane for almost 0.5 mile/800m, but immediately before reaching Lullingstone Roman Villa, turn left on a footpath rising among trees.

Lullingstone Castle is a Tudor mansion hidden behind a red-brick Queen Anne façade. Home of the Hart-Dyke family for many generations, the small flint-walled chapel in the grounds contains their effigies. The house and grounds are open to the public on set days throughout the summer.

Lullingstone Roman Villa dates from about AD100, but was enlarged over some 300 years of occupation to house what was probably an important Roman official. There were baths and underfloor heating, a Christian chapel, and superb mosaic floors on public display now via English Heritage (☎ 01322 863467, **www.english-heritage.org.uk/southeast**).

Above the trees the way continues to climb, and near the head of the slope the Darent Valley Path breaks off to the right. Ignoring this, veer left in a few paces and cross the open brow of a hill with long views over the Darent Valley. Now the path slopes downhill, passes between scrub trees into a dip, then rises on the other side. When it forks take the left branch through a little wooded area and out to a meadow which you cross along its right-hand edge. On the far side the path divides again. Take the left branch (the other is a bridleway) which takes you through a long strip of woodland with a golf course on the left. At a crossing track continue directly ahead through another section of woodland, but when you emerge from this at a paved way on the golf course, turn right towards a car park and the clubhouse.

About 150m before reaching the car park, note a large wooden signpost. At this point turn left on what is part of a circular walk. Aim for a marker post and continue into Upper Beechen Wood where a broad path takes you down a slope, at the foot of which you cross a fairway – beware flying golf balls! Continue up the grass slope opposite, but very soon veer half-left on a path rising through more woodland. At the top of the slope come to crosstracks and maintain direction to a ladder stile and a gate. An enclosed path now leads ahead to a field, which you cross to Redmans Lane at grid ref 510637.

Turn left, and after about 100m bear right on a concrete driveway leading to two bungalows. At the end of the second garden boundary the path bears right into a large field. Keep to the right-hand edge, and at the far corner cross a stile into a sloping meadow, with fine views to the steep scarp slope of the Downs. Hills of woodland and meadow fold into neat valleys ahead.

Descend the scrub-pocked meadow to its bottom left-hand corner where a stile brings you onto a lane opposite a cottage at grid ref 515628. Bear left, following the lane through an avenue of mature trees, then turn right at a T-junction. (Note the interesting memorial stone up a few steps on the right.) Continue up the lane to another junction. Ignore the left turn for Shoreham and stay on the right fork for a short distance. On coming to a cottage on the left, turn onto a track immediately left of the driveway. This track runs above and to the right of a sunken pathway, veering to the right and rising steadily. When it forks at the entrance to Meenfield Wood continue directly ahead, with steep meadows sweeping down to Shoreham on your left.

The way takes you above a large memorial cross cut into the chalk slope, with a dedication to the men of Shoreham who lost their lives in the 1914–18 war. From it there is a splendid view over the village and the Darent Valley. Continue ahead as far as a crossing path where you descend to the village, passing the Shoreham Aircraft Museum where teas are served when open (Sundays from May to September 10am–5pm (☎01959 524416, **www.shoreham-aircraft-museum.co.uk**). Turn right along the High Street, then left into Church Street.

Shoreham is an attractive and interesting village with a number of tile-hung or flint-walled cottages, and a picturesque bridge over the Darent whose stream adds much to its charm. There's a railway station on the London (Victoria or Blackfriars) to Ashford line, and a bus service from Sevenoaks. At the railway station the Shoreham Society has developed an interesting Countryside Centre.

Wander down Church Street past the weather-boarded Kings Arms with its unusual ostler's box, then cross the Darent and bear left by the war memorial. Approaching the entrance to The Water House (where Samuel Palmer the artist once lived) veer left on a surfaced path accompanying the stream. When a foot-bridge allows, cross to the left bank where the continuing route is waymarked for the Darent Valley Path. It comes to a lane, curves right and continues as a footpath along-side the Darent before entering a large field. Keep along the right headland, then cross through the middle of the next field to a concrete farm road. Continue ahead and eventually come onto a country road by some houses. At this point veer slightly left, up steps and into a field where you follow its right-hand boundary for about 500m to Lullingstone Park Visitor Centre.

The River Darent drifts beneath the road bridge in Shoreham

31

WALK 2
Shoreham – Romney Street – Shoreham

Distance	5 miles/8km
Map	OS Explorer 147 'Sevenoaks & Tonbridge' 1:25,000
Start	Church of St Peter & St Paul, Shoreham (grid ref 524616)
Access	Via A225, 3 miles/5km north of Sevenoaks
	Nearest railway station: Shoreham
	Shoreham is served by bus from Sevenoaks
Parking	Public car park in Filston Lane, Shoreham (grid ref 518615)
Refreshments	Pubs in Shoreham and Romney Street (150m off route)

'Everything connected with the village in those happy times,' wrote the 19th-century artist Samuel Palmer of the seven years he lived in Shoreham, 'seemed wrapped about with a sentiment of cosy quiet antiquity, full of association that carried you far back into the pastoral life of Merry England years ago.' There's something of that association today, for the Darent Valley – in which Shoreham nestles between ramparts of the North Downs – is surprisingly unspoilt, having happily been spared the ravages of the M25 whose route had once been proposed to go through it. Both village and valley are among the gems of this corner of Kent, with lots of opportunities for the walker. But Shoreham features only at the start and end of this particular walk, for the Darent is soon deserted in order to cross the eastern wall of the Downs to enter a hidden valley whose existence will surprise newcomers to the area. There are several steep sections of path to negotiate, and it should be noted that near the crest of the Downs the footpath enters a rarely used firing range. Should it be in use, a red flag will be flying if it is unsafe to proceed, and a sentry posted who will let you know when to continue.

From the heart of the village pass through Shoreham churchyard into an open field where you turn left. Walk along the field edge until coming to a crossing path, then turn right. This path soon crosses the railway line and brings you to the A225. Cross with care and find a foot-path sign about 50m to the left. Here you go through a hedge and aim half-left across a field to the opposite scrub boundary, then out to a drive below a house. Cross the drive where the continuing path slants up the edge of the garden and wooded hillside beyond. The way steepens towards the top of the slope, then enters the firing range marked by a flagpole. If a red flag is flying, do not proceed until the sentry gives the go-ahead.

Gaining the crest of the Downs come to a crossing path and bear left. The way eventually eases through woodland and emerges to open fields by a second flag-pole. From the woodland corner proceed straight across the field ahead, in effect making for the far corner. A few paces south (right) of this, enter woods again and begin a steep descent among yew trees.

The path emerges into a surprisingly peaceful valley on the edge of a golf course. Enclosed by hedges and trees for about 100m, you then turn left and follow the continuing path through grassland (beware flying golf balls!) and on to a minor lane opposite a large Dutch barn at grid ref 541631. Crossing the lane the way passes to the right of the barn, and comes to a farm drive where you turn right. Passing a few houses and farm buildings the drive takes you on to Upper Austin Lodge. Do not go up to the house itself, but keep well to its left where a track then leads ahead onto the golf course.

About 500m after joining the track leave it in favour of a path on the left which is flanked on both sides by hedges and trees.

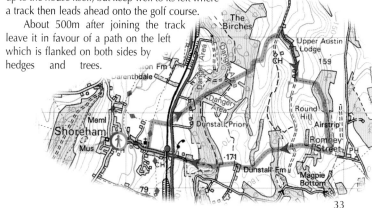

It soon begins to rise up the downland slope towards Lower Wood. Entering a patch of scrub veer right, then left up a sloping meadow. The path then angles along the fence-lined edge of the wood with splendid views ahead, and across to the right where you can see over the brow of Round Hill to the wooded ridge through which the walk had entered this inner section of the Downs. At the end of the fence-line the way continues along the top edge of two linking meadows, until reaching the garden boundary of Romney Street Farm and a crossing path at grid ref 548615. (**Note** If refreshments are needed, cross the stile on the left and walk along the enclosed footpath for about 150m to reach The Fox & Hounds pub in the secluded little hamlet of Romney Street.)

Turn right on the crossing path and enjoy a long view to the right where, far-off, can be seen high-rise buildings along the unseen Thames, which represent a very different world to the one immediately around you! Come to two stiles on either side of a track, and over these descend a steep slope, at the bottom of which you cross a track (part of the golf course again) and continue ahead on another hedge-enclosed footpath. This takes you up a steep slope on the western side of the valley.

Enter woods again, and on emerging from them aim half-left across the corner of a hilltop field. Maintain direction over the next field, then join a crossing track and turn right to reach Dunstall Farm at grid ref 535614. Shortly before reaching the farm the Queen Elizabeth II bridge over the Thames at Dartford can be seen in the distance. Before it lies a tranquil, untroubled landscape. In the farmyard veer right, then left past some barns and cross another open field towards more trees on the lip of the Downs. Shortly after entering Dunstall Woods there's a crossing path. Go straight over this and descend (steeply in places and on a long flight of timber-braced steps) ignoring alternatives to right and left, and come once more into the Darent Valley. Cross the A225 opposite Shoreham station, and wander down the road into Shoreham village.

WALK 3
Westerham – French Street – Chartwell – Westerham

Distance	5 miles/8km
Map	OS Explorer 147 'Sevenoaks & Tonbridge' 1:25,000
Start	Westerham green (grid ref 447540)
Access	On the A25 about 5 miles/8km west of Sevenoaks
	Westerham is served by buses from Bromley and Sevenoaks
Parking	Public car park (fee payable) on A25 east of Westerham near Quebec House
Refreshments	Pubs and cafés in Westerham, tearoom at Chartwell

This circular walk is a real gem that explores some quiet little valleys, woodland, hilltop crests with expansive views, an attractive little hamlet, and wanders alongside Chartwell, one-time home of Sir Winston Churchill. It's a switchback of a route with several steep, though short, ascents and descents to tackle; a fine walk to enjoy in all seasons.

Begin on the triangular village green near Westerham parish church. On the green there's a bronze statue of Churchill by Oscar Nemon, while General James Wolfe holds his sword aloft nearby. Cross the A25 below the Churchill statue and walk ahead down Water Lane, a narrow alleyway that leads between walls, crosses two branches of the Darent stream alongside a neat garden, and enters the foot of a sloping meadow. Walk up the slope to a stile in the skyline fence, after which you cut across a hilltop meadow slightly left, to reach a squeeze stile by an oak tree. An enclosed footpath now takes you to the B2026. Cross with care, turn right, and after a short distance come to a minor junction at grid ref 452533.

Westerham is an historic place whose first inhabitants built their huts within a stockade on what is now the green. In 1227 Henry III granted a charter allowing a market here, thus giving Westerham town status. Among its many fine old buildings there's the 700-year-old Grasshopper above the green, and the Vicarage in which James Wolfe was born in 1727. Wolfe actually spent his childhood in the red-brick, multi-gabled house now known as Quebec House after his famous victory in Canada. This house is now in the care of the National Trust and is open to the public.

Bear left on the lane signed to French Street, but after about 100m break away left along a descending track towards a solitary house, then head to the right on a footpath. In a few paces pass near the entrance to Hosey Cave (barred to keep people out, whilst enabling a colony of bats to fly to and fro). The path winds up among woods and then forks. Continue straight ahead, now out of the woods but going along a tunnel of trees. Just before reaching Gillhams Farm go through a white gate, then turn left on a drive towards stables. The way then swings right and descends alongside a fence, with lovely views left, into more woodland. At the foot of the slope the path crosses a stream and curves right. Shortly after, climb a steep slope on the left by a flight of wood-braced steps, and almost on the brow of the hill turn right on a crossing path. Before long this slopes gently downhill, joins another path and continues ahead before veering right to cross a stream.

Enter a sloping field, go up its left-hand edge to a stile in the top corner where a path now eases along the hillside and emerges (after crossing more stiles) onto a narrow lane in the hamlet of French Street. Immediately before coming onto this lane, note the unusual private burial ground on the right, and a wonderful view left across a valley to the oasthouses of Outridge Farm (see Walk 5).

French Street is a small hamlet tucked among the Greensand Hills

Bear left along the lane past pretty little April Cottage, then turn right on a drive where a bridleway signed Greensand Way takes you alongside the boundary hedge of a house called Mannings Wood. Bear left with the hedge, soon walking along the edge of woodland – the bridleway here can be very muddy in winter, or following heavy rain. Eventually come to a narrow lane. Take the left-hand of two paths directly ahead, which leads down a slope along the Chartwell boundary with views left over a series of small lakes to a vast Wealden panorama.

Home of Sir Winston Churchill from 1924 until his death in 1965, **Chartwell** stands on a high terrace of land overlooking a great sweep of gardens, parkland and lakes, with a splendid view south into the Weald. It was for this view that Churchill bought the house: 'A day away from Chartwell,' he said, 'is a day wasted.' Under the National Trust Chartwell is now part-museum devoted to Churchill's long life and varied careers, and partly the house and home as he knew it for 40 years. Open (not Monday except Bank Holidays) Easter to end of October ☎ 01732 866368.

Come to a country road by the entrance to Chartwell car park. (When the house and grounds are open, refreshments can be had at the tearoom located at the far end of the car park.) Cross the road with care and ascend a steep slope on timber-braced steps to a wooded common. Ignoring alternative paths to right and left, continue directly ahead on the route of the Greensand Way, among bilberry, bracken, heather and rhododendron, with oak, pine and sweet chestnut trees providing almost constant shade. Cross a narrow driveway and in a few paces come to a boundary fence. Turn right and continue ahead at a fork to descend a sunken path leading to the B2026 at grid ref 448515. (**Note** At the fork it's worth making a short diversion onto Mariners Hill. For this veer left and leaving the trees continue between a hedge and a fence to enjoy an expansive view over the Weald.)

Cross slightly to the right and walk down the driveway of another April Cottage; when this curves left into a gateway go ahead a few paces, then left at a junction of paths. Rise up a slope onto Crockham Hill Common, and near the head of the slope come to another path junction. Turn right and follow this path for about 160m, at which point you take an alternative path cutting right through avenues of pine and silver birch, easing downhill and being squeezed at times by rampant rhododendrons as the slope steepens.

An avenue of pine and silver birch takes
the walk across Crockham Hill Common

Emerge below the common to a northward view along Squerryes Park. Over a stile by a field gate walk through gentle meadowland veering half-left to find another stile on the edge of woods. The course of the infant River Darent, which rises in a private garden at the foot of the common, can be seen to the right, while the woods on the left disguise the site of an Iron Age hillfort. The continuing path keeps alongside the woods, and when these end, you come to a dirt track at grid ref 444525.

OPTION A (LAKE WALK)

A few paces along this track cross a stile on the right and walk along the right-hand edge of a sloping meadow, then curve left along a track. This eases through a little valley in which the Darent has been dammed to form three narrow lakes, and makes a pleasant alternative walk without adding any great distance. After crossing two more stiles, the track rejoins the main walk by Park Lodge at grid ref 444536.

MAIN WALK

Follow the track uphill, curving left near the brow of the hill where Squerryes Farm can be seen below. At a junction of paths cross a stile on the right, walk through a wooded grove, over a narrow field and along a fenced path which soon descends steeply, with views of Westerham below and the North Downs ahead, to reach a track by Park Lodge at grid ref 444536.

Walk ahead along the track to a pond seen on the left. On the right a concrete footbridge crosses the Darent stream, with a footpath leading from it along the bottom edge of a sloping meadow. Eventually come to a kissing gate on the left. Through this the way takes you along Water Lane into Westerham opposite the green where the walk began.

WALK 4
Crockham Hill – Toys Hill – Obriss Farm – Crockham Hill

Distance	5 miles/8km
Map	OS Explorer 147 'Sevenoaks & Tonbridge' 1:25,000
Start	Church Road, Crockham Hill (grid ref 443507)
Access	East side of B2026, midway between Westerham and Edenbridge. Crockham Hill is served by infrequent buses from Westerham and Edenbridge
Parking	With discretion in Church Road
Refreshments	None on route, but pub in Crockham Hill

This particular walk is just one of many that could be adopted in this western corner of the county where footpaths abound and broad panoramas capture scenes of great natural beauty. It's countryside that was known and loved by Octavia Hill, one of the co-founders of the National Trust, who walked these same footpaths, fought to keep them open, and now lies buried in Crockham Hill churchyard. Much of the walk has Octavia Hill connections, either through the National Trust, or from more personal association. She lies at rest close to the start of the walk, and within the first mile we pass a cottage she once owned, a seat erected by her in memory of her mother, a hilltop saved by her for the nation, and one of the Trust's most popular properties (Chartwell). At Toys Hill there are woodlands named in Octavia Hill's memory, another cottage once owned by her, and a well that she sank for use by the villagers. As you step out along these paths and enjoy the magnificent views, spare a moment to consider the effect her tremendous vision had on our ability to enjoy open access to this countryside – and give thanks.

Begin on the road leading to the church in Crockham Hill – it is signed from the B2026. Where the lane curves left for the final approach to the church go ahead through a kissing gate beside a field gate, into a meadow at a

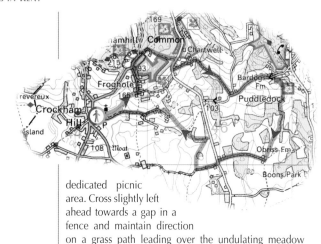

dedicated picnic area. Cross slightly left ahead towards a gap in a fence and maintain direction on a grass path leading over the undulating meadow which was drastically reshaped by a landslip in 1596.

The path brings you to a second kissing gate and a footbridge over a stream. Rise up the left-hand side of the next meadow, then over a stile and up 134 steps between gardens to pass a thatched cottage. Coming onto a lane opposite a converted oasthouse once owned by Octavia Hill, turn left for about 400m until reaching the B2026 shortly after passing Froghole Farm.

Climb more steps immediately on your right, and continue ahead at crossing paths. (The right-hand path

Froghole Farm at Crockham Hill

leads through trees to a seat erected in memory of her mother by Octavia Hill, then continues over Mariners Hill, saved for the nation by Octavia's efforts, where there's another seat with a huge view.) Keep ahead alongside a fence with the crown of Mariners Hill to the right, then veer left among trees. The path curves to the right and forks. Keep to the right-hand option alongside the boundary fence of a solitary house, after which the way begins to lose height, eventually coming onto a country road near Chartwell, home of Winston Churchill for many years, but now open to the public via the National Trust (see Walk 3).

Turn right along the road for a short distance, then cut left on a drive leading to Chartwell Farm. Keeping to the left-hand side of the farmhouse (magnificent rhododendrons and azaleas in early summer), you then pass to the right of two sets of oasthouses and go through a gateway. Ignore the NT-signed paths on the left, and keep ahead, soon veering slightly right on a hedge-lined path that eventually brings you onto Puddledock Lane at grid ref 462509, where you turn left.

Passing the few houses of Puddledock follow the narrow lane uphill towards Toys Hill. A few paces beyond Little Toys (a house on the left), turn right on a short driveway that leads to Bardogs Farmhouse. A footpath now squeezes alongside a hedge left of a gate and continues downhill, curving left then right. Ignoring an alternative which cuts off to the left, our path becomes almost a sunken track before reaching a stile.

Over this wander down a meadowland slope keeping fairly close to the right-hand woodland, to find two stiles at the far corner. Over the left-hand stile walk ahead among trees, then into another meadow. After a short distance go through a line of trees, then aim slightly right ahead over a more open meadowland. On the far side, about 30m from its right-hand corner, cross another stile and continue ahead following the right-hand boundary of a large meadow. Halfway along the boundary come to a barn where you turn right, through a gate and onto a farm track by Obriss Farm. Now walk ahead along the farm drive/track, crossing a ford on the way, and eventually coming to Mapleton Road about 1 mile/1.5km south of Chartwell at grid ref 460501.

> The splendid old farmhouse of **Obriss** is now in the care of the Landmark Trust, from which it may be rented for holiday use.

Turn left along the road for a few paces, then break to the right on a track beside an attractive tile-hung cottage. This track can be notoriously muddy and water-logged in winter – or at any time of year in inclement weather. After about 400m, where it rises and makes a right-hand bend, leave the track to cross a stile on the right into a large meadow from which you have views of the Greensand Ridge, and with Crockham Hill church seen across the fields half-left.

Walk ahead across the meadow towards the left-hand edge of a woodland, and on gaining it keep ahead alongside its fenced boundary, then half-right to another stile. Over this, after a few paces come into another meadow and turn left alongside a woodland shaw. On reaching a corner continue ahead through trees and over yet another stile. This brings you into a sloping meadow where you veer right down the slope to a field gate and a stile by a small stream. Over the stile walk up the next slope, at first alongside its right-hand edge, then on a faint grass path to the head of the slope where there's yet another stile with a glorious view back across the Weald.

The way now continues between hedges and a garden wall, and is soon directed left between fences dividing two sections of garden. Leave this through a white gate, then turn right on a driveway which drops down a slope to the head of a narrow lane. Veer left along the lane, passing a lovely old one-time farmhouse, then between fields, and eventually reach the B2026 in Crockham Hill. The Royal Oak pub is just off to the left, should you be in need of refreshment. Otherwise turn right, and after passing a row of houses, turn right again into Church Road where the walk began.

WALK 5
Toys Hill – Ide Hill – Crockham Hill – French Street – Toys Hill

Distance	9 miles/14.5km
Map	OS Explorer 147 'Sevenoaks & Tonbridge' 1:25,000
Start	National Trust car park, Toys Hill (grid ref 470517)
Access	On minor road (Chart Lane) heading south from A25 at Brasted, midway between Brasted and Four Elms
	Buses serve Ide Hill from Edenbridge and Sevenoaks
Parking	National Trust car park (fee payable)
Refreshments	Pubs in Toys Hill, Ide Hill and Crockham Hill, tearoom at Chartwell

Between the Kent–Surrey border and Sevenoaks, the Greensand Ridge is criss-crossed with numerous footpaths, while the long-distance Greensand Way exploits some of the finest views over the Kentish Weald. Toys Hill, Ide Hill and Crockham Hill are among the highest places along the ridge, while French Street is a delightful hamlet nestling on the northern slope whose valley drains down into the unseen Holmesdale Valley, beyond which stretches the North Downs wall. This walk not only picks out some of the most expansive vantage points along that ridge, but also weaves a route along the lower slopes, going from farm to farm in a surprisingly tranquil landscape. As with Walk 4, this also connects a number of sites associated with the life of Octavia Hill, and the continuing work of the National Trust.

From the entrance to the National Trust car park on the west side of the road on Toys Hill, cross to the east side where a footpath takes you into woodland. At the first junction veer left along the Greensand Way, but at a multi-junction of paths take the second right and soon descend a slope, leaving the woodland at a stile on the edge of an open meadow with big views across the Weald.

There's a
seat on the left
which exploits those views. Turn left round the edge of the
meadow with Ide Hill church seen ahead, and enter a
second meadow. Go down the slope where a stile by a
field gate takes you into a third meadow, at the bottom of
which you cross a footbridge, then go up the slope ahead.
Ascend two linking meadows, and at the top of the second
of these leave the track which continues onto Ide Hill, and
instead take a footpath on the right.

> **Toys Hill** consists of 450 acres/180ha of woodland in
> the care of the National Trust. Those on the east side
> of the road are named after Octavia Hill, one of the
> co-founders of the Trust.

Guided by a fence with more fine views, you soon
enter woodland, cross a small brook and, winding among
trees, start to rise up the steep slope. When the way forks
take the left branch to gain the crown of the hill where

there's an open grass area with three bench seats. (Octavia Hill was directly responsible for saving this hilltop for the National Trust.) Over the hilltop a path continues alongside a fence, then spills out on the village green at Ide Hill, next to the church. On the far side of the green there's a general stores and The Cock Inn.

Turn right on the road in front of the pub, but take great care for there's oncoming traffic and a blind corner. A few paces after passing the village hall (car park and public toilets on the south side of this) come to the B2042, cross with care and turn left. Take the first turning on the right, a narrow lane which forks almost at once. Do not take the upper branch (the Greensand Way), but keep on the lower option, a metalled lane known as Hanging Bank. This curves left then right, and after about 0.5 mile/800m ends by a house. One path cuts off left ahead, but we cross a stile into a meadow rough with hillocks, and another big view which includes Bough Beech Reservoir.

The path between Toys Hill and Ide Hill

47

Cross through the meadow, pass to the left of a pond, then veer slightly left ahead, through a gap, aiming more or less towards a large white house. Wander alongside some bushes, then go through a gate on the right which brings you to a drive at Chains Farm. At the head of this come onto the B2042 again at grid ref 488510.

Walk down the road for about 100m, before turning right onto a narrow lane/farm drive opposite Oakwood Lodge, the large white house seen earlier. The metalled lane eventually takes you past Henden Manor glimpsed through hedges on the right with a moat around it. Go through the farmyard beyond the manor, after which the lane curves left between fields. A short distance after the curve, go through a bridle gate on the right, and along a bridleway that leads from it across a large field. On the far side another gate takes you into a belt of woodland where you descend to the right, curving downhill. Towards the foot of the slope the sunken path often has a small stream running along it. Over a footbridge at the bottom of the slope, the way then rises slightly to pass Tan House, a lovely old tile-hung building in a secluded position.

Now on a drive, follow this to a country road which links Toys Hill with Four Elms, where you turn left. After about 120m turn right on a track which cuts through woodland, then on the other side cross a stile into a narrow meadow. Keep ahead to another belt of woodland. Through this come to a stile beside a bridle gate, then maintain direction along the edge of a second meadow. Over another stile go half-left towards the right-hand end of a barn at Obriss Farm. Here you come onto a farm drive and walk ahead, eventually reaching Mapleton Road at grid ref 460501.

Turn right and walk with care (there's no pavement) along this country road for about 400m. Just after passing a cottage on the right, take a footpath on the left into a belt of trees beside a stream. Soon enter a rectangular meadow and maintain direction along its left-hand boundary. At the far corner go through another strip of trees into a sloping meadow. Veer half-right down to a field gate, a stile and another small stream. Over this walk up the next slope, at first along its right-hand boundary, then on a vague grass path. At the head of the slope cross yet another stile and take the continuing path between hedges and a garden wall. The way soon turns left where fences divide two sections of garden. A white gate then puts you onto a drive. Turn right down this to the head of a narrow metalled lane by a tile-hung cottage.

Follow the lane left to where it feeds into the B2026 in Crockham Hill (the Royal Oak pub is seen a short distance away). Turn right, and after passing a row of houses, turn right again into Church Road. When the road curves left towards Holy Trinity church (Octavia Hill is buried in the churchyard) go ahead through a kissing gate into a meadow at a dedicated picnic area. Cross slightly left ahead towards a gap in a fence, then maintain direction over the undulating meadow with Mariners Hill seen above Froghole Farm and its oasthouses.

The path leads to a second kissing gate and a foot-bridge. Go up the left-hand side of a rising meadow. At the top of this cross a stile and ascend 134 steps between cascading gardens, and passing a thatched cottage emerge onto Froghole Lane. Turn left, and about 400m later come to the B2026 again at grid ref 448514.

Immediately on the right you will see another flight of stone steps, which you now climb onto Mariners Hill. At the top of the steps keep ahead and keep left of a hilltop field. The path soon curves left among trees, and on reaching a corner boundary fence you veer right, then in a few paces break off to the left – now on the route of the Greensand Way.

Mariners Hill was secured for the National Trust by a cheque received by Octavia Hill the day before she died in 1912. With a tremendous panoramic view over three counties (Kent, Surrey and Sussex), a brief diversion to the crown of the hill is worth making.

Cross a narrow drive and continue ahead over a wooded common. Ignoring alternative paths that break off to right and left, eventually descend a fairly steep slope to a lane opposite the entrance to Chartwell. Cross the lane with care onto a continuing footpath immediately left of the car park entrance. It's a narrow, fence-enclosed path from which you gain glimpsed views of the extensive Chartwell grounds. Soon rising among trees you come onto another narrow lane and cross directly ahead onto a bridleway which takes you through more woodland. Once again, ignore alternative paths and keep ahead, eventually curving right alongside the hedged garden boundary of a house at French Street. Very shortly come to a crossing lane within the hamlet at grid ref 458527.

> Home to Sir Winston Churchill for 40-odd years, **Chartwell** is now one of the busiest of National Trust properties. When open, refreshments are available at the house-end of the car park. See Walk 3 for further details.

Leave the Greensand Way here and turn left. Shortly after passing the attractive little white-walled April Cottage, take the right-hand of two footpaths on the right, and descend steeply between fences. At the foot of the slope cross a footbridge over a minor stream, and ascend a rising meadow to its top right-hand corner where there's a stile next to a field gate. Over this turn right on a farm drive, and within a few paces pass along the right-hand side of Outridge Farm, an utterly delightful cottage and oasthouses owned by the National Trust.

Beyond the farm the way brings you to another stile by a field gate, where you maintain direction across a sloping meadow. On the far side come to yet another stile on the edge of Toys Hill woodland. Before entering the woods, pause for a moment to enjoy the view back the way you've come, and as you gather the peace and enjoy the serenity of the scene, remember you're less than 25 miles from Hyde Park Corner! A path takes you

At French Street, below Outridge Farm

up a wooded slope, over a crossing track, and continues uphill, twisting among trees, before coming onto a bridleway track where you bear left. Keep ahead at the next four-way junction, and ignoring alternative paths and tracks you will come to an open space with an information panel on the site of the former Weardale Manor. Continue ahead. The track soon curves left and forks – stay on the main track, but at the next junction take the path which cuts sharply back to the right, for this leads into the car park where the walk began.

Completed in 1906 for Lord and Lady Weardale, **Weardale Manor** had 145 rooms and a 12ft-wide mahogany staircase, but was used by them only in the summer months. Following the death of Lady Weardale, no buyer could be found for the house, and it was demolished in 1939.

WALK 6
Ide Hill – Manor Farm – Ide Hill

Distance	5 miles/8km
Map	OS Explorer 147 'Sevenoaks & Tonbridge' 1:25,000
Start	Ide Hill village green (grid ref 487518)
Access	Via B2042 between Riverhead (Sevenoaks) and Four Elms (Edenbridge)
	Ide Hill is served by bus from Sevenoaks
Parking	Behind the village hall on B2042 south of the village (grid ref 488517)
Refreshments	Pubs at Ide Hill and Whitley Row

Third of that trinity of villages on the Greensand Ridge west of Sevenoaks (the others being Crockham Hill and Toys Hill), Ide Hill is well known to walkers for its generous array of footpaths and magnificent views. Most of the village is grouped near the large sloping green where there's a general stores and a pub, The Cock – said to date from the 16th century – and above the green the highest church in Kent. Yet again, as at Crockham Hill and Toys Hill, there is a memorial to Octavia Hill, co-founder of the National Trust who did so much to save the best of the hilltop viewpoints. For a large part of this walk, views are of the North Downs and Holmesdale Valley, although the return to Ide Hill gives some of the finest views of all over the Weald.

Facing The Cock from the village green, walk along the narrow metalled road which passes to the right in front of the pub parallel with the main road. Curving left you enter a small residential area, at the bottom of which a footpath goes between houses signed to Brook Place. Enter an open field with views ahead to the North Downs, and left towards Toys Hill and the large grey house of Emmetts. At the bottom of the field come onto a drive by a house named The Ramblers and bear right.

The footpath makes a dogleg curve round the outer edge of the garden before striking across more linking fields. Eventually come to a narrow country lane and bear right. This leads to Brook Place, a tall house seen to the right of the lane (grid ref 491529).

Owned by the National Trust, **Emmetts** garden is open to the public, and is especially appealing in bluebell time. For opening times ☎ 01732 751509.

By the entrance to Brook Place stands a black barn, opposite which a track goes between houses and into a field where there are two footpaths. Take the right-hand option rising across the field to a stile on the far side. A few paces beyond this come onto a crossing track and bear left. This soon curves to the right across the misnamed Willow Wood. Keep to the main track as it slopes gently downhill, bringing you to an open field with the North Downs seen ahead broken by the Darent gap.

Go down the right-hand side of this field, cross a stile at the bottom and continue towards isolated Manor Farm. At a crossing track near the farm turn right; it soon becomes a sunken way overhung with trees and studded with bluebells in springtime. Wander up the side of a coppice woodland, and when the path forks, keep ahead. Near the top of the slope join a track on the edge of conifer woods and bear right. Continue uphill to another junction of tracks, then veer left to a definite four-way crossing. Go straight ahead to reach a narrow country road by a house called Forest Edge at grid ref 498531.

From the lip of the Greensand Hills, a view through winter-bare trees reveals Bough Beech Reservoir

Turn right and in 100m come to a minor crossroads by a large triangle of grass. Continue ahead and immediately before reaching a white house (Beech Grove) bear left on a drive, then over a stile onto an enclosed footpath which brings you to another lane. Bear left.

Immediately after passing The Woodman pub turn right. Take the right-hand of two paths, cross a stile and walk across a field aiming slightly right ahead to reach a gap in the trees. Through this another stile gives onto a track sloping downhill. Bear right on a crossing track which leads into Hyde Forest. Keep ahead through the forest, soon rising uphill. When it opens with a field on the left by another crossing track, maintain direction, now with coppice woodland on your right.

Come to a gateway within the forest, and veer right on a footpath that weaves a course among conifers, then brings you to yet another country road. Cross over and

54

take a path half-right along the lip of the Greensand Ridge. When it forks choose the left branch which leads to a ridge projection above the Weald – a superb viewpoint. Head sharply to the right; the path now winds above a steep drop, then parallels the road. Come to a Greensand Way marker and follow paths adopted by this route along the edge of the hills. Cross Yorks Hill Road into the Hanging Bank car park and picnic area (more fine views), then continue with GW waymarks along the crest of Stubbs Wood.

The path eventually swings to the left, slopes down to a driveway, then cuts back to the right above the houses of Hanging Bank, and comes directly to the B2042 on the outskirts of Ide Hill. Bear left to the car park by the village hall, then right into the village proper.

Wealden view from the ridge near Ide Hill

WALK 7
Sevenoaks Weald – Boarhill –
Sevenoaks Weald

Distance	6 miles/9.5km
Map	OS Explorer 147 'Sevenoaks & Tonbridge' 1:25,000
Start	St George's church, Sevenoaks Weald (grid ref 529514)
Access	By minor road signed off A21 south of Sevenoaks
Parking	In a lay-by just north of the church
Refreshments	None on the route

Enjoying a broad panoramic view Sevenoaks Weald lies on the southern slope of the Greensand Hills. The long-distance Greensand Way passes across its northern edge, while numerous other footpaths spread into the Weald or climb onto the ridge to explore a patchwork of woods, fields and meadows. This walk does just that, taking advantage of a quiet agricultural landscape before going up onto the ridge to join the Greensand Way for the return to the village. In winter, or after prolonged rain, some sections may be heavy with Wealden clay, and walkers are also warned that there will be more than 40 stiles to cross on this circuit. But it's a truly splendid walk with many memorable highlights.

Sevenoaks Weald has a large village green at its heart, to the south of which stands Long Barn, one-time home of Vita Sackville-West and Harold Nicolson. In 1936 American aviator, Charles Lindbergh, bought Long Barn, and while there his wife Ann wrote *Listen, the Wind*. The village has other literary associations, for it was also home to that restless poet Edward Thomas who was killed in World War I, and in whose cottage W.H. Davies wrote his *Autobiography of a Supertramp*.

Dale Farm, Sevenoaks Weald

Immediately to the north of St George's church, Church Road meets Glebe Road. A few paces beyond this junction cross a stile on the left next to a field gate. Go down the left-hand side of the field between patches of gorse, then over a brook and up the slope to Dale Farm. Pass along the left-hand side of a converted oasthouse, bear right, then left by farm buildings, and cross another field to a line of trees. Continue over the next field through a fairly new plantation to find a stile among more trees. Veer slightly right ahead to another stile by a field gate, then angle up the slope curving a little to the right to pass the left-hand end of a large barn at grid ref 521512.

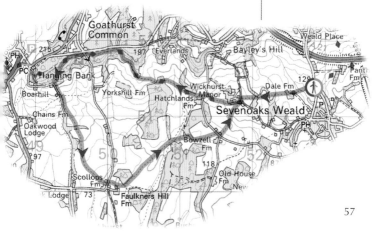

Through a field gate aim half-left towards another line of trees, then down to a farm road where you turn left, then right to pass alongside Wickhurst Manor. Shortly before reaching the end of the farm drive go through a single gate on the left (thus leaving the Greensand Way) and walk across a field to its far left-hand corner where you will find two stiles set among trees. Now follow the left-hand boundary ahead to a third stile, then up a slope aiming slightly left of a house on the brow of the hill where you come onto a country road.

Seen across its lawns, handsome **Wickhurst Manor** has an original medieval hall, and although parts of the building date from the 19th century, the outer wall has a 15th-century stone doorway.

Turn right, and about 40m later cross a stile on the left to pass through a woodland shaw into a large open field. Aiming slightly right across this, meet the far boundary about 40m to the right of Bowzell Wood. Over a stile bear right along the headland of another field. The boundary swings left for a few paces, then breaks off to the right. At this point leave the headland and strike across the field to its bottom right-hand corner. There you cross two stiles and go down the left-hand edge of a field to find another stile in the corner. The path forks. Take the right-hand option, in effect continuing straight ahead along a field boundary to the next corner. The way continues over a stile, then half-left alongside a fence to some trees. Through these cross two linking fields towards the left-hand corner of evergreen woods.

Keep alongside these woods, then over the top left-hand edge of a field, passing to the right of Faulkners Hill Farm where the brow of the hill overlooks valley fields backed by the tree-scragged Greensand Ridge. At the bottom left-hand corner of the field come to a narrow country road opposite cottages. Bear left, and 30m later turn right by a garden hedge, go through a field gate, then left in a garden beyond which you enter a patch of woodland. Over a stream by footbridge, the path then enters an open field at grid ref 499502.

Keep ahead along the right-hand boundary as far as an oak tree, where you then cut half-left through the field to a gap in the far boundary to face a hedgerow separating two more fields. Walk along the left-hand side of the hedge, and at the far end cross a smaller field to a woodland shaw which opens to a large undulating field with Yorkshill Farm, a 15th-century Wealden hall-house, seen half-right across it. Cross half-left to a projection of trees, then wander up the headland to a narrow lane by Boarhill Cottage at grid ref 494514.

Walk up the lane until it curves left. Now take a footpath rising steeply up a wooded slope to gain a crossing path, where you turn right. When it forks remain on the upper level with views looking out to Bough Beech

The Greensand Hills form a backdrop to the view near Faulkners Hill Farm

Reservoir. The path soon rises among trees and reaches another crossing path. Bear right, now on the Greensand Way once more, and follow GW markers at all junctions.

> Created for East Surrey Water Company by damming a valley feeding the River Eden, **Bough Beech Reservoir** was completed in 1969. Bayleaf, a handsome timbered farmhouse, was saved from the waters by being carefully dismantled and transported to the Weald and Downland Museum at Singleton in Sussex, where it was then reassembled. At the reservoir's northern end there's a wildlife reserve, and in a converted oasthouse at nearby Winkhurst Green, the Kent Trust for Nature Conservation has an information centre and a small but interesting hop museum (see Walk 9).

The route traces the edge of the Greensand Hills and brings you to a parking area and picnic site at Goathurst Common. Cross this to its entrance, then over Yorks Hill Road onto the continuing Greensand Way. The path soon forks. Veer left, now parallel with a road, and continue until you come to another marked fork where the Greensand Way branches right and slopes downhill. As in several places, there are impressive views of Bough Beech Reservoir and smaller farm reservoirs at the foot of the slope. Cross a stile and ease round the left-hand boundary of a field to another stile by a gate. Now cross through the middle of an undulating meadow before veering right to enter an oak woodland known as Harbour Hook.

Winding through the woods the path then emerges to meadows which you cross half-right towards Hatchlands Farm, passing alongside another wood. Stiles direct the way round the left-hand side of the farm and onto a country road at grid ref 513513. Turn left, and 100m later cross a stile on the right. Walk down the edge of a large field. Veer left when the hedge ends and cross towards another farm. Here you rejoin the outer route near Wickhurst Manor, and follow the Greensand Way back to Sevenoaks Weald.

WALK 8
Shipbourne – Underriver – Ightham Mote – Shipbourne

Distance	6.5 miles/10.5km
Map	OS Explorer 147 'Sevenoaks & Tonbridge' 1:25,000
Start	Shipbourne church (grid ref 592523)
Access	By A227 about 3.5 miles/5.5km north of Tonbridge
Parking	Along Upper Green Road north of the church
Refreshments	Pubs in Shipbourne and Underriver (120m off route)

The vast expanse and the wooded splendours of the Weald are displayed during this walk. Shipbourne, the village where it begins, lies just below the Greensand Hills that form a protective wall to the north, and this circular outing explores a section of its ridge. But first there are open fields and meadows, the woods and woodland shaws of the Wealden rim to enjoy. There are a few fine houses too, and others perched on the southern slope of the ridge with all the world, it would seem, spread below their gardens. Yet the finest of them all is without question the medieval manor house of Ightham Mote, an architectural gem in the care of the National Trust. This walk passes alongside its moat.

Walk through Shipbourne churchyard and out by way of a kissing gate in the western wall. Take the footpath directly ahead through two adjoining fields, eventually coming to the right-hand corner of a woodland shown as Cold Blows on the 1:25,000 map. Enter this wood and walk ahead up a slope, near the crown of which the path forks. Bear left, still rising among larches. Having gained a high point the way then curves right, eases downhill, and before long brings you onto a narrow country road beside Budds Oast at grid ref 577522.

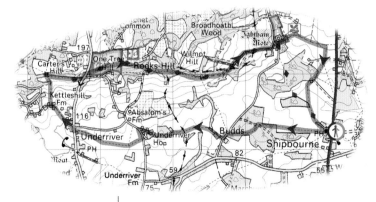

The straggling village of **Shipbourne** is the starting point for several fine walks. At its heart stands the church of St Giles, with The Chaser Inn next door. The church is a Victorian reconstruction with gargoyles projecting from the tower. Note the coffin rest at the lychgate.

Bear left for about 30m before turning right along Great Budds driveway. The path veers right off the drive and cuts along the side of a large black barn. Beyond the garden boundary enter a field with the Greensand Ridge seen to the right. Entering a second field keep ahead to a line of trees, then through these over a couple of stiles towards a pair of barns. Pass along the left-hand side of these and into another field, now with woods on your right and Underriver House seen ahead. At the end of the field there's a stile beside a field gate, where you head to the right towards a second field gate. Do not go through it, but bear left alongside a row of trees, then on a driveway passing a few houses to reach a country road at grid ref 565524.

Turn left, and about 100m later (in front of Underriver House), cross a stile on the right and walk across a meadow to a second stile by a field gate on the edge of a small copse. The way continues ahead, aiming for a pair of oak trees with a stile nearby. Maintaining direction, with splendid views to the right, come to a row of poplars. The footpath goes alongside these and then brings you to another country road at Underriver. (If refreshments are needed, the White Rock Inn lies about 120m to the left.)

Turn right, and after about 100m bear left along a drive by Valley Farm, coloured in springtime with ornamental cherry trees. When it curves right by a house named Black Charles, leave the drive for a bridleway pushing ahead. This narrows on the approach to some converted oasthouses. A few paces before meeting a drive, bear right to pass alongside the oasts, then walk up a delightful sunken path from which you gain snatched views between the trees to the Weald spreading far off, and the Greensand Ridge just above.

Near the head of the slope come to a crossing path, which is part of the Greensand Way, and bear right along it. With woodland on the left and magnificent views to the right, the walk enters its second phase. Soon the views are temporarily restricted, but the path continues and eventually brings you onto a very narrow lane at grid ref 557529.

Emerging from the woods near Wilmot Cottage a broad view is gained over the Weald

Turn left up the lane for a short distance, then bear right (Greensand Way marker) to climb among trees and bushes onto the National Trust-owned One Tree Hill – a misnomer if ever there was one. On its highest point there's a seat with beautiful, far-reaching views. Continue beyond the seat, still following Greensand Way signs, and soon slope downhill among trees, very steeply in places (take care when the path is wet), and eventually come to another very narrow lane opposite Rooks Hill Cottage. Wander down the road a short distance, then bear left on the waymarked footpath.

There are more fine views to enjoy as you maintain direction through sparse woodland at the foot of the steep slope, rich in wild flowers in springtime, and at last you'll come to Wilmot Cottage in a remote location on the edge of woods and with a big view south across the Weald. It is said that the cottage was an alehouse in the days when the trackway past its door was used as a packhorse route. Ignore the path that cuts away to the right (which offers a quick return to Shipbourne via Budds Oast and Cold Blows), and keep ahead, now on a track. This passes between patches of bluebell woods in which there's a mass of wild garlic, and ends at Mote Farm. Bear left at the farm, then turn right on yet another country lane, and in a few paces go left again onto the drive of Ightham Mote.

Ightham Mote dates from around 1320, a magnificent moated manor house now in the care of the National Trust. The Mote of its name refers to its having been a meeting place – or moot – and is not a misspelling of the waterway around it. The house boasts a Great Hall, two chapels, a crypt and a pair of solars, and is well worth visiting. A multi-million pound programme of repair was completed in 2004. For opening times ☎ 01732 811145.

Walk alongside the moat and continue rising uphill beyond the car park entrance, now on a track between fields. It narrows beside a hedgerow and comes to a field

gate with the large grey house known as Fairlawne seen ahead. Bear right along the edge of a meadow and come to a second field gate. Maintain direction, soon sloping downhill to pass along the left headland of a field which borders a cricket pitch. The way continues without difficulty following Greensand Way signs back to Shipbourne churchyard.

A right of way takes the walk past Ightham Mote

WALK 9
Four Elms – Winkhurst Green – Bough Beech – Four Elms

Distance	7 miles/11km
Map	OS Explorer 147 'Sevenoaks & Tonbridge' 1:25,000
Start	The Four Elms pub, Four Elms (grid ref 468483)
Access	Via B2027 about 2 miles/3km northeast of Edenbridge
	On Edenbridge–Tunbridge Wells bus route
Parking	In a lay-by opposite Four Elms church on B2027
Refreshments	Pubs in Four Elms and Bough Beech

Seen from the Greensand Hills to the north, Bough Beech Reservoir appears very much like a natural lake caught in a wooded basin amongst gently rising ground. Indeed, from farmland to east and west a sudden break in a line of hills, or a thinning of trees perhaps, allows a brief glimpse of its watery expanse suggesting it has always been there. Since its creation in the late 1960s it has become an important landscape feature, a place for sailing and birdwatching, with a nature reserve at its northern end where the Kent Wildlife Trust has a Visitor Centre in a converted oasthouse.

This walk makes a circuit of the reservoir, passing the Visitor Centre and an organic dairy farm that has its own brickworks, wanders through meadow and woodland, and alongside a few arable fields by linking footpaths, trackways and hedge-lined country lanes. It's a delightful outing.

From The Four Elms pub walk along the road towards the village church, and in a few paces cross a stile on the left by a field gate. Keep along the edge of a meadow with a stream below to the left. On the far side of the meadow cross a footbridge spanning a drainage ditch, then make for the far right-hand corner of the next field. Go through a gap into an adjacent field and follow the hedge

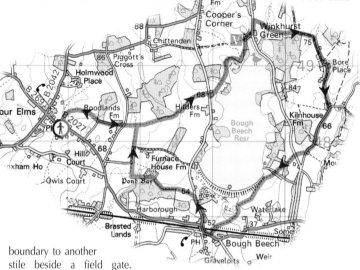

boundary to another
stile beside a field gate.
Maintain direction, but on coming to a
field gate on your left, bear right across the field, then left
to a stile that brings you onto a country lane at an elbow
bend (grid ref 474484). Walk up this lane towards
Roodlands Farm which stands at a T-junction.

Bear left. In a few paces you'll see a field gate on the
right, with a stile immediately to the right of that. Cross
the stile and walk up the left-hand side of a rising field
with views growing in extent as you progress. At the end
of the field briefly bear right, then left through a gateway
and continue ahead alongside a woodland shaw which,
in springtime, has a drift of bluebell and celandine. The
shaw expands into the more extensive Chittenden Wood,
and you pass through a metal field gate to maintain direction beside the wood.

When you reach the end of the wood a stile in the
top left-hand corner of the field gives access to a clump
of trees, where you then cross a footbridge over a little
brook. Ahead can be seen the buildings of Hilders Farm.
Aim half-left across the meadow to a stile in the far
hedgerow. Over this turn right. Eventually come to a gap

where three field boundaries come together. Pass through the gap in the hedge ahead, resume direction, and shortly come onto a country lane opposite a triple-gabled house called Lakefields at grid ref 489486. Bough Beech Reservoir can be seen nearby.

Turn right in front of the house, and on coming to the end of its garden take an enclosed path to the left which brings you within a few yards of the reservoir, then leads into a large field. Follow a line of power cables stretching ahead across the field, and on coming to the corner of Deans Wood, veer half-right to a stile in the opposite boundary hedge. The path now takes you alongside a small reservoir bay where trees stand partly submerged by the water.

The way continues alongside a woodland which is part of a nature reserve, then through a kissing gate to cross a narrow field to a second kissing gate. Maintain direction via linking fields towards the oasthouse of the Bough Beech Visitor Centre at Winkhurst Green (grid ref 495494). Light refreshments are available here when the Centre is open.

On the way to Winkhurst Green the walk edges Bough Beech Reservoir

68

Kent Wildlife Trust has a Visitor Centre in the oasthouse at Winkhurst Green

Leased by Kent Wildlife Trust, the **Bough Beech Visitor Centre** is housed in a 19th-century oasthouse on the edge of the reservoir. Open from 11am–4.30pm between April and October on Wednesdays, weekends and Bank Holiday Mondays, the ground floor of the building has displays about the reservoir and its habitats, while there's a small but interesting museum to the hop industry upstairs.

Walk up the driveway to a narrow road. While bird-watchers gather on the causeway a short distance to the right, we turn left away from the reservoir for about 200m, then enter a field on the right by a gate. Walk along the right-hand boundary with lovely views of the Greensand Ridge to your left. In the bottom corner cross a stream, enter a second field and continue round its right-hand boundary, soon gaining another view of Bough Beech Reservoir.

Towards the end of the field, the line of the footpath angles half-left to cut the final corner, aiming towards a gap on the edge of woodland. Through the gap bear slightly right along a track. Easing gently downhill it kinks to the right and eventually brings you to the complex of buildings at Bore Place.

The Tudor Manor of **Bore Place** is a 500-acre organic dairy farm at the heart of an environmental project founded by the late Neil Wates in 1977 as the Commonwork Trust. Among the enterprises on this 1000-year-old farm is a brickworks using local clay. Educational visits are welcome, and there's a field trail. For further information contact The Commonwork Land Trust, Bore Place, Chiddingstone, Edenbridge TN8 7AR.

Wild cherry blossom hangs over the path at Bore Place

Walk through the farmyard, twisting left at the far end to come onto the driveway which you then follow to the right. It's a long drive, which eventually brings you to a crossing lane between an old forge on the left and a house on the right. Turn right along the hedge-lined lane for about 700m, when you reach a tile-hung house named Hickens. A few paces beyond this cross a stile on the right and walk slightly left ahead over a field towards woodland. Descend onto a road coming from Winkhurst Green, turn right and almost immediately go through a woodland shaw on the left, then aim towards the far left-hand corner of a meadow (which during research was divided into two paddocks).

The way now goes through another woodland shaw. Out of this aim half-right across a field to a driveway used by the Bough Beech Sailing Club. Over the drive maintain direction through yet another woodland shaw with a pond on your left. Now cross a meadow half-right again, towards the dam embankment which obscures the actual reservoir from view. An enclosed footpath then steers the way below the embankment.

> **Bough Beech Reservoir** was created by the East Surrey Water Company in the late 1960s by damming a small valley south of Winkhurst Green. Two of the buildings that would have been inundated by the flooding were dismantled and re-erected at the open-air Weald and Downland Museum at Singleton in West Sussex.

At the end of the enclosed section, a stile takes you through bushes and out into a meadow where you aim half-right once more to find a footbridge on the far side, then maintain direction across a final meadow. There you come onto another enclosed path, this one directing you across the Edenbridge to Tonbridge railway line. **Caution!** Up the bank on the far side emerge beside the B2027 in Bough Beech (grid ref 489468) and turn right.

With The Wheatsheaf pub nearby, follow the road back across the railway line, this time on a bridge. The road then forks. Keep ahead. After about 450m, and just short of a multi-gabled house, cross a stile on the left to walk along the left-hand boundary of a field. Before long cut into the left-hand adjacent field by way of a plank footbridge, then maintain direction alongside the ditch you've just crossed. When the field boundary cuts back to the right, leave it to walk directly ahead to a woodland corner, and continue with Villa Wood now on your left.

On coming to the field corner keep ahead through a woodland shaw and on along the left headland of the next field. At the next boundary corner cross a stile and walk through a charming coppice woodland. The way meanders through, crossing a stream and curving to the right. On emerging from the woodland turn left along the edge of a gently sloping meadow across which can be seen Furnace House Farm.

At the top of the meadow come onto a farm drive and turn right. When it curves right, leave the drive and maintain direction along the edge of fields linked by stiles. At the top left-hand corner of the second field you rejoin the outward walk by a woodland shaw at grid ref 479483.

Turn left through a gateway, then along the right-hand edge of a field before descending to the junction of lanes near Roodlands Farm. Cross almost directly ahead and walk along the lane until it bends sharply to the left. Now over a stile beside a field gate walk ahead a few paces, then right through a gap, and half-left to the far corner of a field. A stile next to another gate takes you into the field ahead where you maintain direction to a gap leading into the next field. Now cut across to the far left-hand corner, over the footbridge and alongside the stream which leads directly to the B2027 near the pub in Four Elms where the walk began.

WALK 10
Marsh Green – Crippenden Manor – Marsh Green

Distance	5.5 miles/9km
Map	OS Explorer 147 'Sevenoaks & Tonbridge' 1:25,000
Start	The village green, Marsh Green (grid ref 439444)
Access	On B2028 1.5 miles/2.5km southwest of Edenbridge
	Nearest railway station: Edenbridge Town (2 miles/3km)
Parking	With discretion beside the village green
Refreshments	Pub in Marsh Green

Marsh Green stands astride the Edenbridge–Lingfield road in the low-lying Eden Valley with views north to the Greensand Ridge. South of the village runs one of those High Weald ridges from whose crown panoramas can be gained of a rolling land of woodland and meadow in which lovely old houses are tucked away in secretive folds and hollows. This walk sneaks into some of those folds, as well as treading the hills that reward with such fine views.

Leaving the village green walk along the road in the direction of Dormansland and Lingfield, and about 150m beyond The Wheatsheaf pub turn left onto the narrow Greybury Lane. Passing a string of houses walk alongside Marsh Green Wood and come to the attractive timber-framed Smoaky Cottage. Immediately past the cottage turn left, and over a stile enter a meadow. Walk ahead along its right-hand boundary with fine views back towards the Greensand Ridge. At the head of the slope cut across to the top left-hand corner where you go through a gateway into a second meadow. Keep along its left-hand edge, and at the far side cross another stile to a fence-enclosed path taking you into woodland.

Passing between ponds come to a crossing path by the boundary fence of Clatfields, go up some steps on the right, over a stile and along the left-hand edge of another meadow. When Clatfields garden boundary cuts away sharply, veer slightly left ahead to another stile, over which you keep left round the edge of a woodland, then over yet another stile into a meadow where you follow the boundary fence ahead. Come to a field gate and a stile into a sloping meadow. Near the foot of the slope cross another stile, then with the woods of Greybury Furzes on your left, walk up the slope to find yet another stile by some barns at Greybury Farm, located at grid ref 438426.

Cross a small fence-enclosed meadow and out by a gate beside a red corrugated iron barn. Now walk ahead along a farm track, and when it forks take the left branch sloping downhill among trees. Having descended into a hollow the way rises again to a pair of farm gates. Pass through the right-hand gate, then veer left in a large meadow. On gaining the upper boundary corner, turn right, still within the meadow, and walk along its top edge towards another woodland. On reaching this, and immediately after passing a pond on your left, go through a bridle gate to enter Ten Acre Wood. The path leads easily through and brings you into the grounds of Crippenden Manor at grid ref 446419.

Crippenden Manor is a large private timber-framed and tile-hung manor of some distinction, built in 1607 and set at the end of a long driveway in the midst of splendid rolling countryside about 1.5 miles/2.5km from Cowden.

Veer left along the bridleway, and on reaching a driveway turn left and follow this for 0.75 mile/1.25km to Gilridge. Having come to a country lane at Gilridge turn left onto another driveway. When this forks take the left branch (directly ahead) alongside The Round House. Go through the gate for Round House Farm, then over a stile on the left where you turn right down the edge of a meadow towards Cobhambury Wood. The way leads into the wood, and shortly after it curves slightly right, the way forks. Turn left down a slope and after a few paces cross a plank footbridge and walk ahead with a stream on your left. (This stretch of woodland is full of bluebells in springtime.)

Still in the woods come to another path junction and turn sharp left down the slope, over the stream and along a narrow sunken path which leads to a stile in the corner of a meadow. Maintain direction and at the top right-hand corner cross another stile beside a farmhouse, then walk ahead along its drive. Ignoring paths breaking to right and left, remain on the drive as far as the entrance to Howletts. Turn left on a bridleway between a fence and hedge, and this will bring you to Shernden Manor. Come onto the drive and walk ahead, passing some very fine properties and with lovely views north across the Eden Valley to the Greensand Ridge. The drive forks. Veer right to pass alongside a large furnace pond, with Christmas Mill on the right, and come to Christmas Place, one-time home of playwright John Osborne at grid ref 444436.

As the drive turns sharp right by Christmas Place, go directly ahead over a stile and along the right-hand edge of a field. Coming to a gap in the hedge, go through to the right, then turn left. Ignoring a stile in the corner, veer right and in the next corner cross another stile and aim slightly left ahead through a large field. Enter the next field ahead, then over a final stile to crossing tracks. Maintain direction along the bottom of some gardens, and come to Marsh Green where the walk began.

WALK 11
Cowden – Horseshoe Green – Bassett's Farm – Cowden

Distance	6 miles/10km
Map	OS Explorer 147 'Sevenoaks & Tonbridge' 1:25,000
Start	By Cowden church (grid ref 466405)
Access	Off B2026 3.5 miles/5.5km south of Edenbridge
	On Edenbridge–Tunbridge Wells bus route
	Nearest railway station: Cowden (1.25 miles/2km)
Parking	With discretion in Cowden High Street
Refreshments	Pub in Cowden

Cowden is protected by a High Weald ridge, from which a beautiful panorama scans north beyond the Eden Valley to the Greensand Ridge and, in places, even beyond that to the North Downs. To the south, in East Sussex, another ridge spreads across the blue horizon. This is Ashdown Forest, one-time royal hunting ground with some fine walks on it (see *Walking in Sussex* also published by Cicerone Press). The following route goes onto other ridge and hilltop vantage points from where long vistas north and south can be claimed, but it is the uncluttered, unspoilt countryside, and a handful of charming old houses that grace it, that will remain in your memory when the walk has been accomplished.

With Cowden parish church on your right, walk along the road as if to leave the village, and just beyond a bus stop go left through a kissing gate into a field. In a few paces the path forks. Take the right-hand option which strikes across the field towards the left-hand side of a white cottage. Cross its drive and continue along a line of trees, then beside Jones's Wood. When the path forks bear right, over a stile and along the right-hand boundary of a field, sloping down to a stream which you cross on a sturdy footbridge. On the skyline can be seen a barn roof.

Angle across the large meadow towards it, passing just to the right of a tree-circled hollow, and find a stile in the top boundary. Over this veer right to a second stile among a group of barns, beyond which you'll come onto the B2026 road at grid ref 467417.

Cross with care to the entrance to Pyle Gate Farm. Go through a gateway and keep right alongside a barn. The way curves left below a house and comes to a crossing track where you turn right. Sloping gently downhill among trees, the track forks at the foot of the slope. Continue ahead for a few paces, but when it curves left towards a secluded cottage, break off to the right on a footpath, still among trees and with a stream below you. After about 180m come to a path junction and turn left uphill, soon passing a railway bridge where the line from the Markbeech Tunnel emerges near Cowden Station.

The branch line from Edenbridge Town to Uckfield which passes through the **Markbeech Tunnel** was built in the 1880s for the London, Brighton and South Coast Railway.

Continue uphill, emerging from the woodland below and to the left of a large red-brick and tile-hung house named Edells. Maintain direction, crossing a squeeze stile in a stand of trees, then up the left-hand side of a sloping meadow to reach a country road named Cow Lane, with beautiful views into Sussex (grid ref 476424).

Turn right along the lane to reach a junction at Horseshoe Green, where you turn

77

downhill in the direction of Cowden Station. About 240m down the lane, just beyond the attractive tile-hung Horseshoe Cottage, enter a meadow on the left. Walk up the slope keeping well to the left of a line of trees, and on coming to a second tree line on the meadow's upper boundary find a stile near its left-hand end by a pond. Cross into the next meadow and walk ahead along its left-hand edge, passing alongside more trees that partially shield another pond. Come to a crossing path and a stile in a gap in the left-hand hedgerow.

Over this stile veer half-right across yet another meadow to a marker post, from which you can see a woodland directly ahead. A stile in the near corner of this woodland carries the path into the trees. Walk along its lower edge – the right-hand slope is honeycombed with rabbit burrows and badger setts, and in springtime a magnificent carpet of bluebells swamps the woodland floor.

Another stile takes you out of the wood, and the continuing path then leads through a long meadow with more woods below and a number of sandstone outcrops above to the right. At the far end of the meadow go through a gap, then follow the left-hand boundary to a stile in the far corner. The path now strikes ahead among trees, then over a narrow stream and out to a final meadow on the far side of which can be seen the handsome old timber-framed Bassett's Farm (built 1622).

Come onto a lane near the house and turn left. This is a most attractive and secluded corner of the county, hidden among wooded hills with ponds and streams in their clefts. After a few paces bear right on a drive leading to Prinkham, another charming old timber-framed house. Just before reaching the house a path cuts alongside the left-hand hedge, and continues to the left of a low barn. On the other side you'll find a stile. Over this veer right round the edge of a field and cross another stile into the adjacent field on the right. Walk through this, parallel with a brook, and come to a sturdy wooden bridge spanning Kent Water, the modest stream that marks the county boundary at grid ref 495408. Cross into East Sussex and bear right.

Even the most common of wayside flowers add beauty to our walks

Over a stile enter a large meadow and follow Kent Water, but shortly after crossing a ditch maintain direction, in effect leaving the course of the stream, then veering slightly left to locate a bridge through which you pass beneath a railway line. Turn right and soon rejoin the stream, going through a succession of meadows linked by stiles and several footbridges provided by Ashdown Ramblers. On reaching a four-way junction of trails, keep ahead to cross a metal bridge into Kent once more, then continue alongside the stream through yet more linking fields.

A footbridge takes you back into Sussex for the last time. Here you walk through an area of paddocks before coming onto the B2026 at the county border. Turn right, then cross with care and enter a field on the left. Remain alongside Kent Water until a field gate with a stile next to it takes the path into another meadow. Again, keep ahead and passing below Sussex House Farm (seen to the left) come to two field gates. Go through the right-hand gate and walk up the edge of a sloping meadow to Cowden church – this cannot be seen until you near the head of the slope, despite its 39m spire. Walk through the churchyard into Cowden High Street.

WALK 12
Cowden – Hoath Corner – Cowden

Distance	8.5 miles/13.5km
Map	OS Explorer 147 'Sevenoaks & Tonbridge' 1:25,000
Start	By Cowden church (grid ref 466405)
Access	Off B2026 3.5 miles/5.5km south of Edenbridge
	On Edenbridge–Tunbridge Wells bus route
	Nearest railway station: Cowden (1.25 miles/2km)
Parking	With discretion in Cowden High Street
Refreshments	Pubs in Cowden and Hoath Corner

Situated close to the border with East Sussex, Cowden lies in the midst of some very fine walking country. The following walk explores some of the best of that countryside, with charming scenery and attractive buildings along a route whose interest never wanes. It begins by following the Sussex Border Path along the banks of Kent Water – the stream that marks the county boundary here – before climbing Hobbs Hill, which looks out on a panorama full of hills and valleys. Skirting Stonewall Park the route drops into a basin almost encircled by hills and woodlands, edges a vine-yard, then cuts across meadows to reach Hoath Corner with its sandstone outcrops and The Rock pub. There are more outcrops and far-reaching views on the continuing walk which takes us to Sandfields Farm, along a lane, then over more fields and meadows on the return to Cowden.

In springtime an abundance of bluebells and wild garlic along stream-bank and hedgerow create a bewitching sight, and when matched against the blossom of wild cherry, crab apple and blackthorn – and the multi-shades of green leaves – makes for a colourful and fragrant outing. Add to that the many different habitats to divert the attention of the amateur naturalist, and it's likely that the walk will take far longer than the actual mileage might otherwise warrant. And why not?

From the bus stop opposite Cowden church, cross the road onto a bridleway/drive which leads to a house.

Go through the yard and onto a grass path along the left-hand side of the house, arriving at a new burial ground east of the church. Take the path ahead (burial ground on your left) and continue down the edge of fields as far as the Kent Water stream opposite attractive Sussex House Farm. Veer left alongside the stream, pass through fields and come onto the B2026 road at grid ref 474405.

Turn right, cross the road bridge into East Sussex, then over a stile on the left to enter a private parking area. The way now leads through small paddocks with the stream on your left, then crosses a footbridge back into Kent. Follow the stream to the right, easing gently through more fields. When you come below the buildings of Moat Farm cross once more to the right bank of Kent Water and continue to follow it downstream, ignoring a second bridge and remaining on the right bank.

Kent Water disappears beneath the bramble-covered embankment of a railway line – if there have been no trains running, you'll barely guess that a railway passes here.

Continue along the edge of more fields, then cut left through a brick archway. Bear half-right to rejoin the stream, and when you come to a footbridge in a field corner, ignore it and continue for a further 50m or so to gain another footbridge, which you cross.

Turn right, once more wandering along the stream's left bank through yet more fields, until you come to a very narrow lane below a house, with Hobbs Hill Farm and oasthouse seen halfway up the slope to the left. Walk up the lane towards it. When the farm drive swings left by the oasthouse, go ahead through a gate and up a sunken track overhung with pine, oak and beech trees. This is a delightful gully of a track, its banks tangled with gnarled roots that grasp the steep slopes on either side. At the top of the slope, where the angle eases, divert for a moment to the left where a splendid view is gained.

The footpath veers to the right along the edge of Hobbs Hill, with more views to enjoy between the trees, then swings left to cross the brow of the hill with fields on both sides. Eventually come to a country road at grid ref 505414. Turn right, and on reaching the minor cross-roads at White Post, bear left. Keep along the road for about 250m, and a few paces beyond the entrance to Finch Green Cottage, you will find a stile on the right giving access to a field in which there are two paths. Aim diagonally left across the field to its far corner, with the large grey mansion of Stonewall Park seen across mead-owland.

Do not go onto the road here, but bear half-right across another field to a gap in a line of trees left of a woodland. Through the gap a path cuts across another open field towards a large house (South Park Farm) seen on the far side. There you turn sharp left to pass along the right-hand side of a group of trees surrounding a pond. Shortly after this the way swings right, then descends stone steps onto a country road. Cross this onto a continuing path that plunges down a slope along the edge of Courtlands Wood. The Greensand Ridge can be seen far to the north, while in the middle distance Penshurst Vineyards stripe the hills.

It was the Romans who introduced the grape to Kent, and in the Middle Ages monks cultivated vines in various parts of the county. In recent times Kent has seen a marked increase in viticulture, and vineyards have become a feature of the High Weald landscape. **Penshurst Vineyards** are open to the public by arrangement with the owners, and Penshurst wines are on sale locally.

The path brings you to a stile. Over this cross a field to a line of trees, and passing through continue down the slope to a footbridge. Continue across the next field to its far corner and a pair of footbridges set at right angles to one another. These deliver you onto the edge of a wood beside a vineyard.

Walk alongside the woodland, bear left round its edge, then over another footbridge turn right through a spinney. The narrow path here can be extremely muddy in winter. Near the head of the slope ignore an alternative path cutting right to Penshurst (see Walk 14) and curve left.

Leaving the trees cross a stile left of a field gate and go straight ahead along the right-hand edge of a field. Maintain direction up a slope towards a red tile-hung cottage where you'll find another stile to its left. The way now takes you through a 'tunnel' of trees and hedges and onto a track/drive. On coming to a timber-framed house, turn right, go up a few steps and ahead along the left-hand edge of a field with big views to the right. At the end of the hedgerow there are two stiles. Cross the second of these and follow the left-hand fence to the top of the field (note rock outcrops half-hidden among trees and bushes). Bear right and soon cross another stile on the left. The continuing path takes you through woodland, then out to a sloping meadow, at the top of which you come onto a road by some houses at Hoath Corner (grid ref 497431).

Turn right for a few paces, then left at a junction of roads with The Rock pub nearby. Passing some very attractive houses and fine views off to the right, follow this road for a little over 0.5 mile (1km) as far as a T-junction. Almost opposite you at this point, note a gate next to the driveway of a house. Cross a stile by this gate and walk ahead along a track.

At the end of the track pass through a gate on the right, then wander half-left across a field to a woodland known as Bilton's Gill. An enclosed path now eases along the woodland edge before curving right and descending to a footbridge over a stream. Up the other side you emerge to a large field. Keep to its left-hand edge, and when the trees finish maintain direction (the brow of the hill to your left) to find a stile in the opposite hedgerow. Over this aim to the left of a pair of cottages and come onto a driveway. Turn left along the drive and wander down to a narrow lane where you turn left once more as far as Wickens Farm at grid ref 484415.

Continue a short distance beyond the farm, then turn right on a footpath along the side of woodland. On reaching a stile maintain direction across a slope to a gateway. (Note the large sandstone outcrop on the left.) Keep ahead to the far side of a field where you then turn right and walk down the slope. Pass through the farmyard at Sandfields Farm to reach a country road by a railway bridge.

Cross the bridge and follow the road for about 600m, passing Moat Farm and a group of houses, and ignoring path options to right and left. Just after passing Moat Cottages the road curves to the right. Leave it here and take a footpath on the left. It crosses a narrow field, then over a stile into a large open field. Keep along its left headland, and on reaching the far boundary, curve right with it. About 100m later cross a footbridge into another field. Walk straight ahead to pass a pond and woodland on your left, then enter another field across which you can see a house on the far side. Aiming just to the left of this, reach the B2026 road at grid ref 474407.

Cross with care to an enclosed footpath leading to a large field. Wander over this aiming half-left to find a stile in an angle formed by the junction of two lines of trees. A series of stone steps (**caution**: slippery when wet) takes

you down to a footbridge spanning a stream running through a little woodland. Leaving the woods cross straight ahead to the corner of a scrubby woodland shaw, through which you then descend to a final footbridge. Heading up the slope beyond will bring you directly to Cowden churchyard.

Cowden church where Walk 12 ends

WALK 13
Chiddingstone – Penshurst – Chiddingstone

Distance	6.5 miles/10.5km
Map	OS Explorer 147 'Sevenoaks & Tonbridge' 1:25,000
Start	St Mary's church, Chiddingstone (grid ref 501452)
Access	Via minor road south of Bough Beech on B2027 Edenbridge–Tonbridge road
	On Edenbridge–Tunbridge Wells bus route
Parking	With discretion in Chiddingstone High Street
Refreshments	Pubs and tearooms in Chiddingstone and Penshurst

Though small, both Chiddingstone and Penshurst count among Kent's most attractive and interesting villages; the first for the simple charm of its street which is lined with half-timbered inn and houses owned by the National Trust, and with its castle seen across a lily-padded lake nearby; the second for the splendour of Penshurst Place which dominates the village and surrounding area. Both are set in gently rolling countryside, much of which is explored on this walk.

With the church on your left, walk along Chiddingstone High Street heading east for about 50m. Ignore the first path on the right with a sign to the Chiding Stone, but take the next a few paces beyond it. Passing alongside a playing field, you soon enter a large open field with views across an expanding countryside – Chiddingstone Castle and church are seen off to the right.

The single street of Tudor houses makes **Chiddingstone** one of the most frequently filmed of all Kent's villages, the half-timbered buildings adding a touch of authenticity to various historical dramas. The Castle Inn has been an inn since 1730; ornate

Oasthouses are a quintessential feature of the Kent countryside; these are at Chiddingstone

gates next to it allow private access to the solemn, stone-encased mansion formerly known as High Street House. Originally a Tudor manor, it was almost completely demolished in 1679 by Henry Streatfeild, who then set about building a red-brick replacement. A century later the whole edifice was given a stone and battlemented façade with fanciful turrets and towers, and renamed Chiddingstone Castle. The church of St Mary is surprisingly spacious to serve so small a parish, while the Chiding

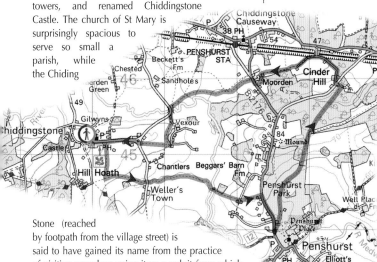

Stone (reached by footpath from the village street) is said to have gained its name from the practice of visiting preachers using it as a pulpit from which to chide the locals for their sinful ways.

Cross the field, sloping down towards a group of trees encircling a pond, where another path cuts sharply left. This leads to the opposite boundary and a stile by a large oak tree. Continue over the next field, making for its far right-hand corner where you come onto a country road by a field gate near a sign announcing Wellers Town, at grid ref 507446.

Turn right, but in a few paces cross another stile into a field on the left. Walk along the left headland, then through a gap into the next field. Continue ahead along the left-hand boundary, eventually coming to a stile by a field gate. A few paces after crossing this, bear left over a stream, then veer half-right towards an arched footbridge spanning the River Eden. Across this turn right along the end of a woodland (Clappers Shaw), then left up a slope, at the top of which you'll find a pair of Dutch barns. Continue ahead, now following the right-hand boundary of a field. Reaching the corner descend some steps onto the B2176 road and walk down it (**caution**) towards Penshurst.

After 400m pass a lodge by a private drive on the left. A short distance beyond this cross a stile into the grounds of Penshurst Place, then cut sharply left across a brief parkland corner. (Should you be in need of refreshment, continue along the road to find a pub and two teahouses.) Go through a squeeze stile and over the drive to a second section of parkland. Keeping left of a cricket pitch, locate a stile situated about 100m left of a fence surrounding a lake known as Lancup Well. Entering a new parkland section bear right alongside the boundary fence until another squeeze stile provides access to yet another area of enclosed parkland. (Note the ancient half-dead oak tree surrounded by fencing nearby; it is said that the last bear in England was killed here.)

The mellow walls of **Penshurst Place** stare out across the parkland, the west side defended by a ha-ha, the south partly hidden by a wall that surrounds a garden, of which Ben Jonson wrote: 'Then hath thy orchard fruit, thy garden flowers, Fresh as the ayre,

and new as the houres.' A house stood here at the time of the Domesday Book, but it was Sir John de Pulteney who in 1340 set the foundations of the present Penshurst Place. Its most impressive feature is the Great Hall, 60ft high with a chestnut-beamed roof. Elizabeth I was a frequent visitor, for Sir Philip Sidney (1554–86), the poet and statesman who was one of her favourites, was born here. The house is open to the public and repays a visit.

The walk goes through the parkland of Penshurst Place

Come to an avenue of trees, then bear left up the slope between them to a stile near a magnificent specimen oak tree whose large branches are held aloft as if to support the sky. At the top of the slope veer right for a few paces, then go left along the edge of a plantation through the right-hand of two rectangular grassed areas, towards a large wood consisting mostly of conifers. A clear track leads through, but on reaching a crossing track on the far side, bear left to gain a country road at grid ref 534459.

Turn left, then almost immediately head to the right on a narrow lane which leads alongside Roundabout Wood. When the lane makes a sharp right-hand bend over the railway, walk ahead on the drive of Little Moorden. A short distance along the drive cross a stile into the right-hand field, then wander along its left-hand edge. At the far side maintain direction through a hop garden, then follow a track into a farmyard. Bear left and come to the B2176 at Moorden Farm.

Turn right, then left over a stile into an undulating meadow. Walk directly ahead, and at the end of this meadow go down a slope and veer right through a gap, then left to a field gate and another stile. Walk ahead across the next meadow to locate a stile in the far hedgerow about 30m to the right of a pillbox. Cross to another gap in the far boundary, enter the next low-lying meadow and make for the far left-hand corner where a footbridge takes the way across a stream into yet another meadow. Ahead to the left can be seen Vexour Bridge which spans the River Eden. Cross to this bridge and come onto another country road at grid ref 512456.

Over the bridge walk up a private drive for a short distance. The drive curves left immediately after passing a clump of trees disguising a hollow. Here you break off to the right on a path which rises into a field. Bear left along its headland, and on reaching the brow of the hill, turn sharp right across the centre of the field towards oasthouses seen through some trees. On the far side come onto a lane by a pond. Turn right, then left in front of a handsome group of converted oasts at a triangle of roads, and walk into Chiddingstone.

WALK 14
Penshurst – Salmans – Nashes Farm – Penshurst

Distance	5.5 miles/9km
Map	OS Explorer 147 'Sevenoaks & Tonbridge' 1:25,000
Start	Opposite Penshurst Place on B2176 (grid ref 526439)
Access	Via B2176 about 4.5 miles/7km southwest of Tonbridge
	On Edenbridge–Tunbridge Wells bus route
	Nearest railway station: Penshurst (2 miles/3km)
Parking	Lay-by on B2176 400m north of village centre
Refreshments	Two pubs on the walk, plus pub and tearoooms in Penshurst

Best known for the impressive 14th-century Penshurst Place (open to the public), Penshurst stands on a slight rise above water meadows at the confluence of the Eden and infant River Medway in a sprawl of farmland. It's a fertile landscape of folding hills, steep beechwood hangers, splendid buildings hidden in remote corners, and a veritable wonderland of footpaths and trackways by which to explore it. On this walk we have distant views of the Greensand Hills, and others that look onto the snaking Medway. In springtime the woods and hedgerows are banked with wild flowers; in summertime the valleys and their walling hills create a tartan of textures; in autumn the beechwoods are a glorious kaleidoscope of colour; but during the winter the low-lying fields and meadows transform this countryside into a mini Lake District.

Begin at the northern, uphill, end of the lay-by parking area (opposite Penshurst Place) where a farm drive cuts back to the west signed to Salmans Farm. When the drive swings left shortly after crossing the River Eden, keep ahead on a track rising gently. Near the top of the rise you can see oasthouses at Chiddingstone ahead to the right, backed by the distant Greensand Ridge. On reaching Wat Stock Farm the track forks. Take the left

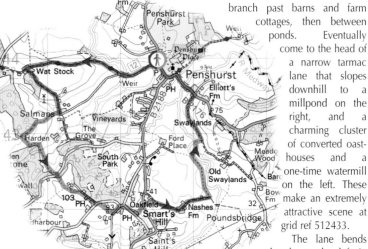

branch past barns and farm cottages, then between ponds. Eventually come to the head of a narrow tarmac lane that slopes downhill to a millpond on the right, and a charming cluster of converted oast-houses and a one-time watermill on the left. These make an extremely attractive scene at grid ref 512433.

The lane bends sharply to the left in front of Salmans Farm, at which point go through a kissing gate on the right and along a broad grass path. After going through a second kissing gate the path ascends some wood-braced steps and alongside a fence through a meadow. Pass through a third kissing gate, walk ahead a few paces to cross a stile, then turn right along the edge of another meadow. Maintain direction along the top edge of a vineyard in whose corner a stile takes the path among trees. In a few paces come to a crossing path and turn left.

This narrow path is squeezed by trees and scrub (muddy in winter), and it slopes downhill before swinging left into the bottom of the vineyard. Leaving this at the foot of the slope beside a pond, cross a couple of footbridges and walk ahead. Another footbridge over a brook leads into an undulating meadow which you cross, passing a line of trees, to a stile opposite. Over this the way veers left along the foot of a wooded slope before rising by a flight of wood-braced steps onto a lane at grid ref 511425.

Cross to some stone steps which take you onto an open hilltop field, and there maintain direction, passing along the left-hand side of a tree-girdled pond with South Park Farm ahead. Walk along the field boundary, then cross a stile near a trig point and continue between fences. This leads directly to a drive where you turn right, and soon come onto a country lane beside The Bottle House Inn.

Bear left for a few paces, then cut right on a continuing path among trees which leads to Nunnery Lane. Turn left. At a T-junction of lanes turn right. **Caution** is advised. At another junction a few paces later keep to the right-hand lane (direction Fordcombe and Tunbridge Wells) and soon reach The Spotted Dog, a 15th-century pub almost hanging from a steep slope, with a fine view across the valley of the infant Medway. Take a footpath on the left just after the Chapel House, and descend along the edge of a sloping meadow to the B2188 at grid ref 523422.

About 40m to the left you'll see a footpath sign directing the way into a field alongside a house. This path soon comes onto a drive where you turn right and wander on to Nashes Farm. Immediately before the farmhouse veer left and take a continuing track which is then bordered by hedges. When the hedges give way and the track enters a field, turn left along its edge, then feed into the adjacent field through a gap. Joining the River Medway remain in the field and follow the river downstream as far as a footbridge.

Cross the river and go round the left-hand edge of a field. This in turn leads into another on the left. Keep to the upper edge alongside the low boundary wall of Swaylands School, and you'll come onto a track with Penshurst Place and church seen ahead. When you reach a road (the B2176), follow this into the heart of Penshurst. Shortly after passing the group of old half-timbered cottages that form Leicester Square (through which the churchyard is entered) come to a junction of roads by the Quaintways Tearooms and turn right. The lay-by parking area where the walk began is a short distance along this road. On the way you will pass another tearoom and public toilets.

WALK 15
Penshurst – Fordcombe – Penshurst

Distance	7 miles/11km
Map	OS Explorer 147 'Sevenoaks & Tonbridge' 1:25,000
Start	Leicester Square, Penshurst (grid ref 527437)
Access	Via B2176 about 4.5 miles/7km southwest of Tonbridge
	On Edenbridge–Tunbridge Wells bus route
	Nearest station: Penshurst (2 miles/3km)
Parking	Lay-by on B2176 400m north of village centre
Refreshments	Pub and tearooms in Penshurst, pub in Fordcombe

This walk explores the upper valley of the Medway. It's a peaceful valley cupped between gentle curving ridges from which footpaths provide memorable views. Fordcombe, which marks the turning point of the walk, sits close to the border with East Sussex. Without being overtly picturesque, it is nonetheless a cheery village with some very fine countryside spreading from it; an altogether pleasing collection of village green, school, pub, playing field and a string of typical Kentish houses. Linking the two villages, the walk enjoys many fine intimate scenes as well as wide panoramas.

With your back to Leicester Square walk down the road beyond the archway entrance to Penshurst Place, continue along the B2176 and cross the Medway. Beyond the river the road rises. Immediately after passing a house on the right named Holly Bank, turn along a track to enter fields.

Named after the first Earl of Leicester, the group of timber-framed houses that enclose **Leicester Square** make an attractive scene. Through the Square you enter the churchyard whose sandstone church is 800 years old, and contains an impressive number of memorials to the Sidney family of Penshurst Place.

Curving leftward the track narrows to a footpath tracing the top edge of two linking fields. A low wall on the left marks the boundary of Swaylands, a stone-built Tudor-style mansion used today as a boarding school. On reaching the end of the second field cross a stile in the corner and continue ahead, soon to gain a view of Old Swaylands, a timber-framed house with a large pond in the dip before you. Beyond it the Medway's valley stretches between converging hills.

Come onto a track that leads to a driveway, then turn right. Walk past the entrance to Old Swaylands (grid ref 534426) and along the left-hand side of a black weatherboarded house. The next house is named The Ring Time, and opposite it, on the left, you'll find a stile which takes you into a small meadow. Walk ahead to a gate, and through this a few more paces bring you to a second gate leading into a field. Now go half-right across this and a second field. Entering a third field bear half-left to locate a stile in the boundary hedge, over which you come to a hop garden. Turn right along its edge and shortly reach a stream. Just to the left a footbridge takes you over the stream where you then wander across a meadow to reach the River Medway by a sturdy footbridge at grid ref 533421.

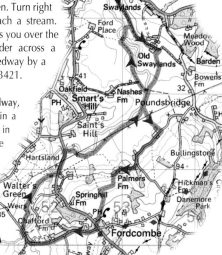

Kent's major river, the **Medway**, has one its earliest sources in a black bog on Ashdown Forest in Sussex, and forms the county boundary between Groombridge and Ashurst. It then cuts right through Kent to its estuary beyond Rochester. The river is tidal as far as Allington, near Maidstone, and navigable from the estuary to

Tonbridge. Between Tonbridge and Rochester the Medway is accompanied almost continuously by a towpath that offers fine walking opportunities. See Walk 19 for a sample.

Do not cross the bridge but follow the river upstream through linking meadows. On coming to a stile and a short plank footbridge spanning a deep little watercourse, cross with care (especially if wet) and bear left. Now follow a line of trees to the top end of a meadow where you then kink right and left, and rise through an enclosed woodland shaw to a narrow country road beside some houses. Turn right, and shortly pass Hamsell Farm at grid ref 535415.

Walk along the road for about a third of a mile (550m), ignoring a footpath on the left. The road bends sharply left by some cottages, and forks soon after. Take the right branch, a rough drive leading to Palmers Farm. Go through the farmyard, cluttered as it is with old machinery, but on coming to some tile-hung cottages on the right of the drive, turn left up some steps and cross a stile in a hedge. Bear half-right up a sloping field, then pass through a gap by a holly tree in the upper boundary. Continue up the left-hand edge of the next field, then turn right along its top edge. In the far right-hand corner of this field you'll find a stile on the left – but before crossing this, note the far-reaching views back towards the north where the horizon is outlined by the Greensand Ridge.

Over the stile ignore another on the right and continue up the right-hand edge of the field towards its top corner. Before reaching this, however, a stile on the right brings you into a hilltop field with Fordcombe church seen on the far side. Wander through the middle of this field, making for the far corner where there's a gate and another stile beneath an oak tree near some houses. (More magnificent views behind.) Now go ahead between gardens to reach the B2188 opposite Fordcombe primary school at grid ref 527403. (About 50m to the right you'll find The Chafford Arms pub and a telephone kiosk.)

Being grouped above the Medway, with Sussex hills mingling with those of Kent nearby, **Fordcombe** enjoys a very pleasant location. There are plenty of good local walks; the Wealdway passes through, and the Sussex Border Path makes a bypass round it.

Cross to Chafford Lane and follow this for about 0.75 mile (1km). Initially passing a cricket pitch, the lane descends past a few houses and a mobile home park. Ignoring paths to right and left, at the foot of the slope come to Chafford Bridge which spans the River Medway. The river here snakes through a pleasant valley with the Sussex border a short distance upstream.

Over the bridge leave Chafford Lane for a footpath on the right. Keeping company with the river wander through meadows, soon passing a flood barrier. On reaching a footbridge cross to the right bank, then bear left to the B2188 road. Walk along the road towards a hump-backed bridge, but note the footpath cutting through meadows on the right, which eventually joins our riverside path. Immediately before the bridge leave the road and follow the right bank of the Medway downstream, tracing the headland of several fields for about 1 mile (1.5km). Eventually you come to the plank footbridge over the deep watercourse crossed on the outward route. Over this continue alongside the river for a short distance, then cross to the left bank on a sturdy bridge at grid ref 533421.

Walk ahead to the far side of the first field, then bear right and go through a large gap into the next field. Now follow the Medway's left bank until you come to another bridge. Here you cross to the right bank once more, then veer left round a field edge, soon joining the outward path which you follow to the left. The way becomes a track curving right and leading to the B2176. Turn left into Penshurst.

WALK 16
Groombridge – Speldhurst – Groombridge

Distance	7 miles/11km
Maps	OS Explorer 135 'Ashdown Forest' and 147 'Sevenoaks & Tonbridge' 1:25,000
Start	The Crown Inn, Groombridge (grid ref 531377)
Access	Via A264 and B2110 about 4 miles/6.5km west of Tunbridge Wells
	Groombridge is served by bus from Tunbridge Wells and Crawley
Parking	Public car park opposite the post office (grid ref 531374)
Refreshments	Pubs in Groombridge and Speldhurst

Groombridge is unequally divided by the little River Grom, an early tributary of the Medway and a symbolic boundary between Kent and East Sussex. South of the Grom Sussex claims by far the larger part of the village, but the older and undeniably more attractive portion is grouped around a sloping, triangular green below The Crown Inn on the Kent side of the stream. Weatherboarded or tile-hung cottages create a charming scene, while nearby stands Groombridge Place, a Charles II manor house with open parkland, a moat and a lake to reflect a bank of rhododendrons. Apart from the village, the countryside in which it is set has an appeal all its own, with long views and intimate corners, quaint cottages, ponds, streams, bluebell woods, and folding hills and vales. In short, a quintessential High Weald landscape.

Cross the B2110 by The Crown Inn, go through a gate and along a footpath beside a churchyard. Entering parkland the way is clearly defined, leading across a drive, along the edge of a lake and round the side of the moat which surrounds Groombridge Place. Ignore a path breaking to the right (it leads to the car park) and continue ahead, through a gate and across a large field. On the far side maintain direction with a river on your left, cross a foot-bridge spanning a ditch and continue ahead along the right-hand side of a row of pollarded willows. The way then veers left towards the farm buildings of Pokehill. Across the farm drive the path bears left

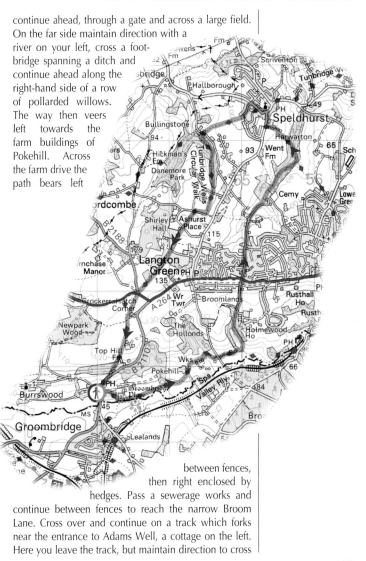

between fences, then right enclosed by hedges. Pass a sewerage works and continue between fences to reach the narrow Broom Lane. Cross over and continue on a track which forks near the entrance to Adams Well, a cottage on the left. Here you leave the track, but maintain direction to cross

Groombridge straddles the border with Sussex

a bridge over a minor stream, then bear left on a sunken path rising among trees. Eventually come to Barrow Lane and follow this to the A264 at Langton Green (grid ref 550392).

> **Groombridge Place** occupies the site of a Saxon castle built by Gromen, after whom Groombridge takes its name. Gromen's castle was replaced by a Norman structure, while the present building dates from the early 17th century. The very fine gardens are open to the public.

Cross the road with care and walk along Farnham Lane, initially lined with houses, then easing into countryside where Speldhurst church may be glimpsed some way ahead. About 0.5 mile (800m) from the main road, a minor lane cuts left towards Speldhurst. Ignore this and continue for another 300m. As the lane curves to the right, leave it by way of a stile on the left and walk down a sloping meadow to a stream. Across this veer slightly left to pass round the foot of a hill, then over another stile into woodland. At a crossing path keep ahead, walking parallel with the stream; later the path is joined by another from the right. You then curve left easing uphill where the path forks. Take the left branch, and soon cross the stream by footbridge. Rising up the opposite bank you then come out of the woods and along a footpath enclosed by hedges. This leads to a drive which eventually opens onto a road. Turn right towards the parish church in Speldhurst.

> **Speldhurst** is an old village, first mentioned in a document dated AD768. Built on a High Weald ridge on the edge of a former iron-making region, it's an attractive village with several pleasant buildings, among them the church of St Mary the Virgin. Noted for its windows by Burne-Jones and William Morris, the church is a Victorian replacement of the Norman original that was destroyed by fire after being struck by lightning in 1791. The half-timbered George and Dragon Inn nearby is said to originate from the 13th century.

At a T-junction in front of the church turn left. The road curves to the right, and about 100m later you take a path on the left, marked for the Wealdway and Bullingstone Lane. It keeps alongside a wooden fence and leads into a large field where the path is enclosed by wire fences and you gain big views to the west and south-west. Across the field enter a long woodland shaw which brings you to Bullingstone Lane. Bear right to pass an old farmhouse, then turn left immediately before a lovely little thatched cottage (Old Bullingstone), where a footpath leads into Avery's Wood, and then forks.

Branch left here and shortly cross a stream following marker posts showing signs for the High Weald Walk through the wood. On coming to a distinctive Y-junction, take the right fork. This path soon rises gently and leaves the wood through a gate, then continues on the left-hand side of a meadow. At the far side a stile has been created out of a tree trunk. Over a drive leading to Danemore Park, go ahead along the left-hand side of a second meadow, and at the far corner cross a stile on the left, then bear right alongside the field boundary to gain a country road at grid ref 545401.

Turn right. Ignore the first path on the left, and almost 200m after coming onto the road, and just before reaching the entrance drive to Danemore Farm, go through a kissing gate on the left and wander across a field to a second kissing gate and a squeeze stile. Maintain direction over a meadow towards a brick-built barn or stable. The way continues across the drive to Shirley Hall (a white building seen to the right), goes through more gates and along the right-hand edge of a meadow with a sports ground off to the left. Cross a second drive (to Ashurst Place), and continue to follow High Weald Walk waymarks through linking meadows.

At the junction of A264 and B2188 by Langton Lodge (grid ref 535390), cross both roads, then over a stile walk ahead through a large field towards the right-hand side of houses. A series of gates direct you leftwards and on to a major track where you turn right. In a few paces the track forks and you take the left branch which leads to Top Hill Farm – with fine views on the way.

At the right-hand end of farm buildings come onto a farm road which soon gives way to a footpath running along the left-hand side of a field and into woodland. This is magnificent with bluebells in springtime. Winding downhill the path brings you onto the B2110, where you bear right and walk into Groombridge.

WALK 17
Brenchley – Matfield – Brenchley

Distance	7 miles/11km
Map	OS Explorer 136 'The Weald' 1:25,000
Start	Brenchley church (grid ref 680417)
Access	By minor road off B2160 east of Matfield, about 2.5 miles/4km southeast of Paddock Wood
Parking	Opposite Brenchley post office
Refreshments	Pubs in Brenchley and Matfield

If one ever needed convincing that the Weald of Kent justifies the epithet of Garden of England, this walk should do it. Orchards, hop gardens and fields of soft fruit are all visited on this circuit, while the villages of Brenchley and Matfield have a number of attractive houses set in a lush countryside. Matfield is especially fine, with a charming village green and duck pond. During research some orchard sections on the route were being grubbed out, while others were being replanted; a reminder that the agricultural landscape is constantly evolving.

Brenchley's church stands among neatly clipped yew hedges on the southern side of a three-way junction of roads at the eastern end of the village. A minor road, Windmill Hill, projects north of the small triangle of grass, and the walk begins on a walled tarmac path which cuts to the right alongside the timber-framed Town Farm Cottage.

> Brenchley's little triangle of grass formerly housed the village pound. The poet Siegfried Sassoon lived in the village and wrote about the area in *The Weald of Youth*.

When the path makes a left-hand bend, go ahead over a stile and down a sloping field towards a small woodland. From the foot of the slope climb uphill along

103

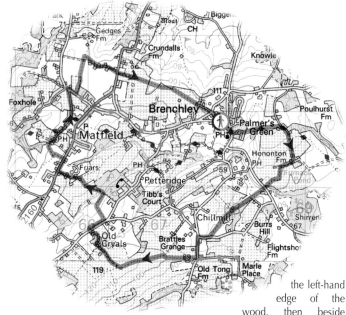

the left-hand edge of the wood, then beside orchards as far as a narrow lane at Palmer's Green (grid ref 686418). Turn right, and walk along a driveway leading to Hononton Farm. At the end of the drive turn right to pass the timber-framed farmhouse, then keep ahead on a track alongside more orchards.

Eventually reach a gap in the shelter belt of trees, and bear left beside another protective row of trees. At the orchard's bottom edge turn right and continue as far as a road by the entrance to Saxby's at grid ref 684410. Opposite stands an attractive house by a pond. Bear right and almost immediately cross the road to a farm track. Just beyond some low buildings cross a stile on the left by a cattle grid, then turn right along the edge of a field.

In the far corner there's another stile and a choice of paths. Ours continues ahead along the lower edge of a wood, soon passing alongside a pond with more orchards stretching up the slope on the far side. Out of the woods the way keeps ahead, and is then guided between fences with another pond on the right, before coming to Spout Lane. Bear right to reach a T-junction, where you turn left and walk along Tong Road.

Near the top of the slope, just after a lane cuts left, turn right on a driveway to pass a bungalow, then enter an orchard on the right. Turn left along its boundary, and on reaching the end of the first orchard section bear right for a few paces, then left to continue through a second orchard. At the far side there's a gate, beyond which you aim half-left through an old orchard (during research part of this was being grubbed out) towards the far left-hand corner. About 30m to the right of that corner you will find a stile, over which you walk ahead alongside a large shelter belt of trees between more orchards.

Come to a track and follow this ahead. It soon curves right on its way to Cryals Farm. A tarmac drive continues from the track, and when it forks in front of large packing sheds, bear right along the driveway that curves round the end of the sheds and brings you to Cryals Road at grid ref 661404. Cross the road, enter a field by way of a stile, then turn right along its edge. At the next corner come onto a track and bear left. Near the bottom of the track, just before reaching a small lake, cross a stile on the right and walk along a fence-enclosed path. At the end of this is a crossing path where you turn left. Passing the end of the lake keep on until you reach a concrete drive. This in turn leads to the B2160 on the outskirts of Matfield at grid ref 656412.

Turn right. About 200m later cross the road to a stile beside a field gate. Walk across two small paddocks, and on entering a larger meadow bear half-right round its boundary until you come to another stile which leads the path to a drive just beyond a splendid converted oast-house. Follow the drive to Matfield village green, and maintain direction along its left-hand side. (For refreshments turn right. There are pubs beside the main road on either side of the village green.)

On the northern side of the green keep ahead along the continuing lane out of the village as far as a road junction. Turn right, but after about 120m enter a small wood on the left where a clear path keeps near its left-hand edge. On emerging from the wood maintain direction alongside a hedge, and as you progress with currant bushes running in lines across the field, so big views grow to the north over the Medway's valley.

Crossing a narrow farm track, keep ahead for a short distance, then turn right beside a line of poplars heading towards oasthouses, with those splendid views now to the left. The footpath brings you onto a driveway, which leads in turn to the B2160 again, at grid ref 664426. Cross the road half-right to another farm drive. When this curves sharply to the left, bear right through a gap, then follow a footpath between hedges. Beyond the hedges maintain direction through more orchard country, soon passing just left of a farm reservoir. Beyond the reservoir

Matfield's large village green is graced with a pond

the way continues along the edge of linking orchards, but about 100m or so before reaching more converted oast-houses, veer slightly right, then left to a drive beside a house.

When you reach a second drive take the footpath on the right, then resume direction parallel with the driveway as far as a junction of roads. Here you go half-left and wander down Holly Bank, the road which brings you to the heart of Brenchley by the war memorial. Turn left for the church and car park.

On the return to Brenchley the walk passes several oasthouses

WALK 18
Yalding – Hunton – Buston Manor – Yalding

Distance	6.5 miles/10.5km
Maps	OS Explorer 136 'The Weald' and 148 'Maidstone & the Medway Towns' 1:25,000
Start	Yalding church (grid ref 698501)
Access	Via B2010 about 6 miles/9.5km southwest of Maidstone
	Nearest railway station: Yalding
Parking	With discretion in Yalding's main street
Refreshments	Pubs and shops in Yalding

Contained on the north bank of the River Beult, near its confluence with the Medway, Yalding has some attractive buildings and verdant hills rising from it. It was this countryside of which William Cobbett wrote so enthusiastically in his classic *Rural Rides*: 'The ten miles between Maidstone and Tonbridge I believe to be the very finest, as to fertility and diminutive beauty, in the whole world... There are, on rising grounds, not only hop gardens and beautiful woods, but immense orchards of apples, pears, plums, cherries and filberts, and these, in many cases, with gooseberries and currants and raspberries beneath.'

Spread along the Greensand Hills facing the sun, these fertile slopes are visited on this walk. It begins, however, by heading eastward below the hills, crossing along the edge of Hunton Park among woodland and low-lying fields punctuated with oasthouses. Then the walk strikes away to the north to ascend orchard-clad slopes, gaining big panoramic views of the Weald across acres of spring blossom. Then it follows the Greensand Way back along the crest of the hills before descending through a tunnel of trees to Yalding once more.

Walk through Yalding churchyard to the left of the church, then turn right along a track which passes to the rear of the local primary school, and a graveyard

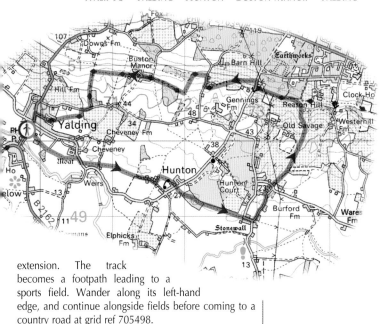

extension. The track becomes a footpath leading to a sports field. Wander along its left-hand edge, and continue alongside fields before coming to a country road at grid ref 705498.

Turn right, and shortly after, ascend stone steps on the left to enter a field. The path cuts diagonally across to the far right-hand corner where a stile brings you onto a drive. Cross this and continue ahead on an obvious track edging several fields. Eventually it brings you to Grove Farm, where there are some converted farm buildings, one of which is an oasthouse. Keep ahead on the surfaced drive for about 100m, then bear left on another track, passing an old barn. About 80m later veer right along the edge of what was an old orchard. In the far corner turn right on a short stretch of path, then left by garages, soon to reach a road in the little village of Hunton at grid ref 719494.

Across the road go through a swing gate into a meadow, and veer slightly left to a woodland, where you will find a stile. Over this a path leads through the woodland, then out into a corner of Hunton Park which you

Yalding's main street is lined with a number of attractive houses

cross to another stile about 100m away. As you cross towards it, the grey building of Hunton Court may be seen off to the left.

> **Hunton Park** covers about 100 acres of grassland and woods. The 13th-century church of St Mary, and the ragstone Hunton Court, both stand within it. Hunton Court is a somewhat plain 18th-century house once owned by Sir Henry Campbell-Bannerman, one-time Prime Minister.

Having left the park, the way now follows its boundary fence, and continues beyond it. Maintain direction along a line of trees to a narrow country lane near some oasthouses. Follow the lane round to the right, passing an early 15th-century timber-framed house, shortly after which the lane forks. Take the left-hand option, signed to Linton, and after about 500m you arrive at a T-junction beside Foresters Cottages at grid ref 733494.

A footpath sign opposite directs the route along the side of Elm Corner Cottage and into a long woodland shaw. Come out of the trees and maintain direction, working a way up the slope among orchards, and passing well to the right of Old Savage Farm. As you gain height so views back across the Weald become more expansive. At the top of the orchards veer left along the boundary until you reach a corner where the path goes into a coppice. Almost immediately bear left on the Greensand Way which hugs the coppice edge, and eventually slopes into the top of more orchards.

Continue in the same direction to the far corner, then descend a steep flight of steps onto the sunken narrow lane of Hunton Hill. Go up the lane with caution for about 100m, then bear left into yet more orchards. Keep ahead along the hillside, then descend through a gate to the lower edge of a bank and resume direction. Enormous views entice you on. Ahead, you'll see a collection of oasts and converted farm buildings. On reaching them the path swings left then right round the garden boundary, and along the driveway to another country lane at grid ref 723507.

Turn right and walk uphill for about 120m to find a track on the left. Along this cross a stile and walk ahead alongside a young woodland for about 150m, then descend on steps to the lower field and turn right – still following the Greensand Way, which leads to Yalding.

When the boundary breaks away to the right, go downhill through the field, heading south towards the valley. Come to a crossing track and turn right. Passing Malice Wood continue to a complex of farm buildings, which forms part of the Buston Manor estate.

Buston Manor is an L-shaped medieval house which displays clear evidence of various additions and alterations. It overlooks a great sweep of countryside.

Walk through the farmyard and ahead on a driveway, then downhill onto a track to pass below Buston Manor. The track takes you between large fields,

Orchards above Yalding

and on coming to a dividing hedge a Greensand Way sign directs you along its left-hand side. At a crossing track enclosed by trees, turn left. This is a bridleway, a lovely sunken track leading down to a country road. Turn right, and in another 150m take a fenced path on the left which eventually brings you round the edge of gardens and out to a residential street. A few paces later a path heads left beside the first house. This leads to another residential street. Bear right for a short distance, then left on a footpath from a parking bay. Passing attractive almshouses, the path brings you out near the main street in Yalding.

WALK 19
Teston Bridge – Wateringbury – Kettle Corner – Teston Bridge

Distance	5.5 miles/9km
Map	OS Explorer 148 'Maidstone & The Medway Towns' 1:25,000
Start	Teston Bridge Picnic Site, Teston (grid ref 708533)
Access	On B2163 just off A26 about 3 miles/5km west of Maidstone
	Nearest railway station: Wateringbury
	Teston is served by the Maidstone–Tunbridge Wells bus
Parking	At the picnic site (fee payable)
Refreshments	Pub and café/restaurant at Wateringbury

Teston Bridge is one of four medieval ragstone bridges on the Medway – the others are at Yalding, East Farleigh and Aylesford. Nearby a lock, a weir and the remains of an old oil mill reflected in the river form a picturesque group. The picnic site comes down to the river at this point. Consisting of 30 acres of water meadows, a car park, public toilets and several rustic picnic tables, it is extremely popular with families, anglers and walkers in the summer, and on fine weekends throughout the year.

On this walk the Medway towpath is followed upstream as far as Bow Bridge at Wateringbury. After crossing the bridge there's a change of direction, with the route heading downstream before veering away from the river to West Farleigh church and Kettle Corner, below which the Medway is rejoined for a return to Teston Bridge. On this gentle, undemanding walk there's a possibility of catching sight of kingfisher or heron along the river; snipe and tern can also sometimes be seen.

Leaving the car park cross the picnic site to the riverside and turn right along the towpath which almost at once takes you alongside Teston Lock. The path is without complication and after about a mile (1.5km), and shortly before coming to Bow Bridge, there will be plenty of river craft moored alongside.

Teston Bridge is one of four medieval ragstone bridges to span the Medway

Teston Lock was originally built in 1740 by the Medway Navigation Company, and rebuilt in 1911. The weir next to it was once used as an eel trap, while the ruins of Tutsham Mill opposite are a reminder that linseed oil was once produced here. The mill was destroyed by fire in 1885.

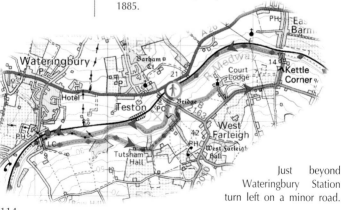

Just beyond Wateringbury Station turn left on a minor road.

(For refreshments turn right to The Railway Inn, or cross the road ahead to the Riverside Restaurant.) Cross the bridge to the south side of the river, then cut left to a stile next to a field gate. Over this walk ahead through a low-lying meadow to a kissing gate giving access to a second meadow, where the continuing path is led by a fence. On the far side a footbridge spanning a ditch takes you into a third meadow. Enter the lower edge of Waregraves Wood with the Medway now curving close by – note that since crossing Bow Bridge the way has been following the Medway Valley Walk.

Leave the wood over a stile, and about 100m further on, veer a little to the right to rise round a shoulder of hillside following a line of marker posts across meadowland. These lead to a grey Dutch barn and a track that continues to converted farm buildings near Tutsham Hall at grid ref 706526. At the top of the slope cross a stile on the left, and come onto a metalled drive which you now follow as it sweeps round the hillside, with fine views overlooking Teston Lock and the Medway.

The River Medway at Teston Lock

Pass alongside a row of white weatherboarded cottages, then continue along the drive as far as the B2163. While the Medway Valley Walk descends to Teston Bridge (and a quick return to the picnic site, if needed), we cross the road directly ahead, go up a few steps and along a fence-enclosed footpath among trees. At the end of the fenced section turn right and walk along the headland of a rectangular field, at the top of which bear left. On reaching the next corner cross a stile and maintain direction, ignoring the alternative path which cuts off to the right.

Pass along the edge of a cricket ground, which has an attractive thatched pavilion, and come onto a metalled lane near West Farleigh church. Turn right and walk up to the B2010 Yalding to Maidstone road (grid ref 716534), then turn left. There is a pavement along which you can walk as far as Kettle Corner, just past an East Farleigh sign, where St Helen's Lane breaks to the left between houses.

All Saints church, West Farleigh dates from around 1100, although the Domesday Book records a church being here before that. Next to it stands the handsome half-timbered Court Lodge Farm.

Descend along the lane to the river and cross to the north bank. The lovely old Barming Bridge, also known as Kettle or St Helen's Bridge, which formerly stood here, was the only timber bridge on the Medway, but this was dismantled in 1996 and replaced by a temporary footbridge. Over this bear left and follow the towpath through pleasant meadows back to Teston Bridge.

WALK 20
Linton – Boughton Monchelsea Place – Linton

Distance	5 miles/8km
Maps	OS Explorer 136 'The Weald' and 148 'Maidstone & the Medway Towns' 1:25,000
Start	Linton church (grid ref 755502)
Access	Via A229 south of Maidstone
	Linton is on the Maidstone–Cranbrook bus route
Parking	Public car park immediately north of the church
Refreshments	Pub in Linton

Linton enjoys a suntrap position on the slopes of the Greensand Ridge south of Maidstone. Overlooking the Weald, with the River Beult curling sedately at the foot of the slope, the panorama includes uncountable acres of orchard and fruit field as though this were one vast market garden – the Garden of England. To the east stretch greenswards of parkland. Then more orchards, more parklands, and fruit fields and orchards again. To the west a bewildering complexity of fruit trees adorn the slopes leading to Yalding and countryside explored on Walk 18. There are oasthouses, farms, a few barns and tile-hung cottages that punctuate these bountiful acres, while the glint of sun on water betrays the river below, and one or two farm reservoirs.

This walk is a joy; gentle and undemanding, with only one short uphill section to face. It comes into its own in blossom time, when there's a delirium of colour and fragrance, with bees thundering in the orchards, and those great commanding views framed by nature's seasonal burst of extravagance.

Wander through the churchyard of St Nicholas heading east, away from the road, and enter the grounds of Linton Park. The path strikes across the parkland, goes over a drive (the massive white house may be seen to the right)

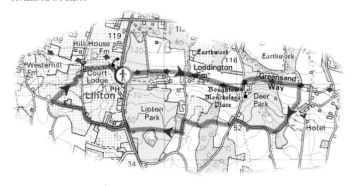

and maintains direction on the waymarked Greensand Way. Passing behind a ragstone house, continue across Loddington Lane and beyond a converted oasthouse, soon to regain views over the Wealden expanse.

> Built in the 1730s by Robert Mann, **Linton Park** enjoys a huge view. Horace Walpole likened it to '...the citadel of Kent, the whole county its garden'.

The stumpy tower of Boughton Monchelsea's church is seen ahead, as is the farm-like entrance to Boughton Monchelsea Place, although the house itself will not be seen for some time. Just before coming to a road bear left when the path forks. (The alternative leads to the church, from whose doorway a magnificent view overlooks a deer park.) Our path curves among trees, crosses Church Lane and continues through a patch of coppice woodland to a car park.

> Boughton Monchelsea village lies to the north of the church, its quarries providing much of the ragstone for local building purposes. The L-shaped **Boughton Monchelsea Place**, which dates from 1567, is a prime example of a mansion built of this Kentish ragstone.

From the car park walk ahead through a large meadow, on the far side of which the path goes along the top edge of a field that sweeps down into the Weald, with splendid views again. When you gain the far boundary, turn right and walk downhill (there's an orchard on the left, beyond the boundary hedge, with Wierton Place beyond that). Continue down the slope, passing a Dutch barn in the neighbouring field, and soon come to a fence which encloses Boughton Park. Walk down the left-hand side of this fence, and about 250m below the Dutch barn, cross a stile on the right leading into the parkland. Turn half-left to resume downhill.

At the foot of the slope a small tree-encircled lake flows into another, smaller, pool, with reeds lining the interlocking stream, while off to the right fallow deer may be seen grazing the parkland beyond a high deer fence. Pass along the left-hand end of the smaller pool, then strike half-right to a gate with a stile beside it, at the left-hand end of the deer fence. Over the stile come onto a lane at a bend (grid ref 774495).

Walk up the lane for about 500m, with views through the deer fence up the sweep of parkland to Boughton Monchelsea church and the ragstone mansion. Come to a T-junction and turn left. After passing Church Farm Barn (a barn conversion) bear right on a footpath running alongside the garden boundary hedge. At the far right-hand corner of the field a plank footbridge carries the path over a ditch, before entering Darnold Wood. The woodland is full of wild flowers in springtime: primrose, celandine, wood anemone, bluebell and early purple orchid. Marker posts direct the way through, although the path is clear enough.

Out of the woods go down a grass slope, over a brook and into an orchard. Through this come onto a lane and bear left. As you wander down the lane, there's another woodland to your right which ends at a fenced enclosure, after which you turn right on a footpath leading into Linton Park. Walk directly ahead along a fence-line, with the great white mansion seen to the right among stately trees and shrubs. Pass alongside a lake and maintain direction to reach the A229 below Linton village. Cross the road with care, turn right and take the first turning on the left. This is Wheelers Lane (grid ref 755495), which you follow for about 0.5 mile/800m.

At first this is a residential street, but houses make way for orchards and a view west along the slope of the Greensand Hills. At Toke Farm the lane curves to the right, and through orchards a fine view may be had to Linton church. The lane forks soon after, and you take the left branch, Barnes Lane. After about 250m leave it for a footpath on the right, beside Bramley Cottage. Walk up the right-hand edge of an orchard, and on reaching its upper boundary cross a stile and bear right, now slanting uphill towards farm buildings. Keeping these to your left, come onto a lane flanked by a tall cypress hedge, and turn left.

The hedge/windbreak ends at a farm drive where a footpath sign indicates the way to Linton church. Follow the drive between orchards with a magnificent panoramic view. Caught by sunlight this curving hillside is a wonderland of colour and artistry; an immense patchwork of orchards – the fertile land put to productive use. After passing Little Court, a solitary peach-coloured house on the left, climb a flight of steps and continue into the car park of The Bull Inn, almost directly opposite Linton church.

The final stage of the walk returns to Linton alongside orchards

WALK 21
Ulcombe Church – Boughton Malherbe – Grafty Green – Ulcombe

Distance	7.5 miles/12km
Map	OS Explorer 137 'Ashford, Headcorn, Chilham & Wye' 1:25,000
Start	Ulcombe church (grid ref 847498)
Access	The church is 0.5 mile/800m north of Ulcombe on a minor road (signed) running south of A20 east of Leeds Castle
Parking	By the church – please avoid service times
Refreshments	Pub and shop in Grafty Green (Ulcombe also has a pub, not en route)

As is true of much of the Greensand Ridge, magnificent panoramic views over the Weald are enjoyed for long sections of this walk, which for the first part follows the Greensand Way eastwards. It then returns through lush Wealden countryside as far as Grafty Green, before rising onto the Greensand Hills via their southern flank.

From the Norman church of All Saints at Ulcombe, cross the road heading east where the Greensand Way is directed onto a footpath alongside a building, then down the side of a sloping meadow, wet from a number of springs that rise nearby. Enter and pass through a small woodland with a pond on the left, then go up a slope with broad views opening to the right. A stile leads into another field where you continue to a row of poplars. Walk along their left-hand side, then continue over a meadow to another stile on its far side. Over this descend a few steps, then head uphill to a narrow road at grid ref 857497.

The attractive ragstone church of **All Saints** at Ulcombe dates from Norman times when, according

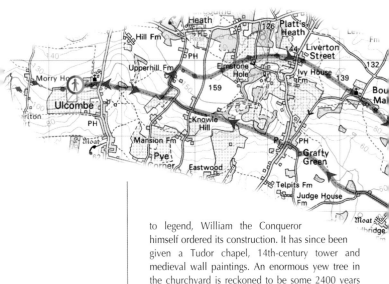

to legend, William the Conqueror himself ordered its construction. It has since been given a Tudor chapel, 14th-century tower and medieval wall paintings. An enormous yew tree in the churchyard is reckoned to be some 2400 years old.

Turn left along the road for about 300m, passing between Upperhill Farm and Weald View Farm, then go through a gap on the right and walk across a hilltop field to a dividing line of trees. The path goes along the right-hand side to a very narrow lane, then through another gap into the field ahead, where you cross to the far left-hand corner. Enter a woodland area of hazel coppice which, when in leaf, is like walking through a tunnel of foliage.

Coppicing (from the French word *couper*, meaning 'to cut') is a form of woodland management where after trees are felled, their stumps – or stools – are left to produce new shoots which grow much faster than trees begun from seed. By this method, a single tree can be harvested many times, and some coppice woodland may therefore be hundreds of years old.

On coming to a narrow driveway bear left, then right a few paces later on the continuing Greensand Way along the edge of a hazel platt (the name for an 'orchard' of hazelnuts), then into an orchard of fruit trees. A stile in the far corner gives onto yet another narrow lane at a bend. Continue into more orchards where you aim half-left between rows of fruit trees. Passing through a gap in the opposite hedgerow the way now crosses an extensive region of bushes and trees, then along an enclosed path at the bottom of gardens in Liverton Street.

Cross the road, go up some steps and ahead on a footpath by Churchill Cottage, soon to gain snatched views between trees into the Weald. Coming out of an enclosed section to a large field, there's a vast uninterrupted panorama – ahead can be seen Boughton Place, with Boughton Malherbe church tower beyond farm buildings. Entering the farmyard, bear right through it, then left along a road to the church at grid ref 883495.

Boughton Malherbe church

123

Boughton Place was once part of a much larger Elizabethan mansion built for the Wotton family. In his biography of Sir Henry Wotton (who described an ambassador as an 'honest man sent to lie abroad for his country'), Izaak Walton wrote that Boughton Malherbe has 'the advantage of a large Prospect'. Which it still has.

Beyond the church the road curves left, with a minor lane (a driveway) dropping to the right. Go down this driveway, but reaching a gate near a pond below The Old Rectory, cross a stile onto a footpath which parallels the drive. (Another path forks right, but we ignore this.) Go through a gate into a meadow and continue directly ahead. Just beyond a small barn enter a large sloping meadow, and veer a little to the right. Not only does the meadow have a number of small hollows in it, but wonderful panoramic views. Make towards the left-hand end of a small copse seen on the far side, halfway down the slope. There you cross another stile and walk towards the right-hand side of Pope Hall Cottage, where the path goes alongside the garden boundary on the edge of a large field.

The path cuts through the field and along the northern edge of Coldbridge Wood. On reaching its eastern end bear right on a rutted track. After a few paces the Greensand Way breaks left over a stile, but you ignore this and remain on the track which edges the wood heading south and is likely to be waterlogged in inclement weather.

When the wood finishes, the track keeps ahead between hedges and trees, and about 150m later is crossed by a footpath (unmarked during research). Bear right through a gap in the hedge and strike across a large open field to its far boundary where you will find a plank footbridge over a ditch with a stile leading into another field. Walk ahead, aiming half-left to a field gate by an oak tree. Come onto a country road and turn right.

After about 600m the road bends sharply to the left by Roughets Wood. Leave it here and take a footpath along the left-hand side of the wood, then enter the next field ahead. The way keeps along the right-hand boundary (cowslips alongside the ditch in springtime), then enters the adjacent field on the right through a gap, and resumes direction. When the hedgerow makes a sharp right-hand turn, cross a stile and walk ahead along the left-hand edge of the next field. Continue through a gap into a final field and following its left-hand boundary towards Ash Tree Farm, come to a field gate leading onto Woodcock Lane at grid ref 875487.

Bear right, to reach a road junction at Grafty Green. Nearby you'll find a pub and post office stores. Turn left, and in a few paces take a footpath on the right beside an electricity sub-station, then alongside a bungalow and ahead through its garden to a stile in the top boundary. Now walk uphill aiming half-right to a woodland, and bear left alongside it. At the field corner cross a stile, and when the wood cuts back to the right, maintain direction to another stile found among a line of trees.

The way continues among trees and bushes beside a fence to rise above a farm reservoir. On reaching a farm track follow this ahead, gently rising and eventually coming to a junction of lanes. Walk directly ahead to pass the half-timbered Knowle Hill Cottage, soon gaining more splendid views before reaching a T-junction. Cross to a footpath descending among trees (**caution** when wet), then keep ahead along the right-hand edge of a small meadow. At the far side bear left for a few paces to find a stile, over which you cross a field to its far left corner and rejoin the outward Greensand Way. Retrace the outward route back to Ulcombe church.

WALK 22
Pluckley – Little Chart – Egerton – Pluckley

Distance	6.5 miles/10.5km
Map	OS Explorer 137 'Ashford, Headcorn, Chilham & Wye' 1:25,000
Start	Pluckley playing field (grid ref 926455)
Access	Via Pluckley Road, about 3 miles/5km southwest of Charing Nearest railway station: Pluckley (1.5 miles/2.5km)
Parking	With discretion in the village
Refreshments	Pubs in Pluckley, Little Chart and Egerton

A major part of this walk follows the Greensand Way on a linking of three villages, making a circuit that exploits wide vistas over a peaceful agricultural land. Each of the villages holds something of interest, while the countryside itself is most attractive with an array of orchards erupting with blossom in springtime.

In Pluckley's main street linking Smarden with Charing, about 100m north of the Bethersden turn-off, a Greensand Way signpost directs the start of this walk into the village playing field on the eastern side of the road. Cross to the far side, and about 20m from the right-hand corner, enter an orchard and walk ahead through it. Continue through a succession of orchards, passing alongside the beautiful garden of Sheerland Farm. Soon after, come to a narrow lane and maintain direction alongside a wall, then over a stile and along the left-hand edge of a field.

Enter another orchard and wander directly through it, with glimpsed views of the North Downs to the left, then over a stile in a shelter belt of trees. Veer left round the edge of yet another orchard, then right at the

The walk passes alongside the garden of Sheerland Farm

boundary corner. About 20m after this corner, go through a gap on the left and walk through the next orchard (between the trees) to its far side where a waymark post then directs you to the right-hand corner boundary. Going through a gap Little Chart church is seen ahead. The path crosses a field towards it and brings you to a road left of the church, opposite The Swan Inn at grid ref 944459.

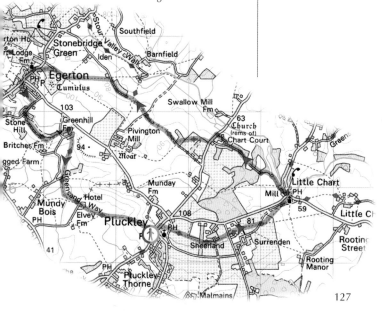

The 13th-century church of St Mary's was destroyed by a doodlebug in 1944

Built of brick, and resembling a water-tower, the neo-Gothic **church of St Mary** in Little Chart was consecrated in 1955 as a replacement for the original medieval church (almost 1 mile/1.5km away) that was destroyed in World War II. A number of houses in the village have distinctive arched windows that give the appearance of quizzical eyebrows. These are typical of all buildings of the Dering estate – see note below about Pluckley.

Bear left, and at a T-junction a few paces later, cross directly ahead on a track leading into a field – now on the route of the Stour Valley Walk. A footpath edges the right-hand boundary from which it may be possible to see one of two millponds through the trees on the right. Curve left with the field edge, then turn right with the continuing footpath which soon joins a track alongside fields, woods and more orchards.

Come to farm buildings with a ruined church tower seen ahead. Now on a concrete farm road, take the right-hand option when it forks, and shortly after veer left towards a group of oasthouses. A path runs along the right-hand side of the drive leading to these oast-houses, then takes you into the churchyard of St Mary's, whose shell of a tower remains a symbol of the medieval church that once stood here. Pass alongside the ruins and come onto a road at grid ref 934466, then turn left.

The ruined **church of St Mary** dates from 1200. Standing on raised ground above the road, it was destroyed by a doodlebug (flying bomb) on the evening of 16 August 1944. Now only the shell of its tower, and a few skeletal walls, remain to create a romantically attractive scene.

Shortly after passing Chart Court Barn and Chart Court Stables, the road curves slightly. Here you take a footpath on the right which keeps to the edge of a field, then continue into a second field and angle half-left through it, aiming for the right-hand corner of Little Pipers Wood. The path now weaves its way through the wood (masses of bluebells and wild garlic in springtime), and emerges onto a track known as Nettlepole Lane. Turn right.

This track provides lovely long views to the North Downs as it eases between fields, then comes onto the very narrow Pivington Lane at grid ref 924469. Turn right, then left onto a continuing track which soon leads alongside a small woodland. Shortly before reaching Iden Farm Cottage come onto a narrow lane. Leave the lane alongside the cottage garden boundary, then slant across a large field towards Egerton church.

On the far side of the field cross a stile in a hedge and turn left. Through a gate by a water tank turn right, then walk along a track for about 250m. A footpath on the left now angles across a field towards a line of trees that appears left of the church. Cross two stiles within this line of trees, then go half-right to a third stile in a paddock, and across the paddock to its left-hand corner. The way continues along the back of buildings and onto a drive which leads into Egerton's main street opposite the handsome ragstone church at grid ref 908475.

> **Egerton** is gathered at a T-junction of minor roads with fine views south over a sudden slope that drops to the low meadowlands of the Weald. Crowning the village the grey tower of the church of St James is topped by a small turret, a feature common to a number of churches in the Kentish Weald. On the southern edge of the village, enjoying the Wealden view, the Millennium Hall is a handsome building designed to look like a Kentish barn, and is one of the county's finest village halls.

Rejoining the route of the Greensand Way, turn left and walk through the village, soon passing The George Inn with glorious views ahead. A few paces beyond the pub Egerton primary school is seen on the right. Opposite this the Greensand Way breaks to the left along Elm Close. Ignoring a sign which sends a footpath down a slope near the village hall, go as far as the first bungalow on the right at the end of the Close. A path cuts down the side of this and takes you round the headland of a field, then onto a narrow lane. Turn right, and about 200m later, bear left at the entrance to Stone Hill Farm. Pass a converted oast-house, then veer slightly right on a descending concrete farm road with more splendid views to enjoy.

At the end of the concrete a footpath continues ahead, tracing a natural hillside terrace and curving left above Britcher Farm. Through gates or over stiles, the way continues round the edge of fields, before climbing a short flight of steps to a country lane. Wander downhill with yet more wide views ahead. The lane bends to the right. Turn left by a rough drive in front of Greenhill House. Over a stile on the right, turn left and walk down the field edge to a second stile. Across a ditch bear right to yet another stile, then walk along the right-hand edge of a large field divided by fences. On the far side come to a gate and a stile giving access to a meadow in which there's a brick-walled barn.

Bear right on a track, and a few paces later pass through another gate and over a stile on the left. Now keep to the left headland of a field, but about two thirds of the way along it, cross a plank footbridge on the left, then go half-right across a field corner to yet another stile. The way continues across a field towards Elvey Farm, then through the farmyard (this is now Elvey Farm Country Hotel) to a gate leading into a meadow. In the far right-hand corner go through another gate, and after about 30m veer slightly right, then left to maintain direction.

Soon pass through another gate on the left, but continue in the same direction along the right-hand field boundary. When this cuts back to the right, veer slightly right uphill to a bridle gate in a fence-enclosed field below a red tile-hung house. Through the field come to another bridle gate below and to the right of a line of Scots pine trees, and continue along the lower edge of a sloping meadow to a stony drive. This brings you into Pluckley where you bear left to complete the circuit.

Attractively set among orchards on a brow of the Greensand Hills, **Pluckley** is said to be one of the most haunted villages in England. The church of St Nicholas dates from the 13th century and is built of Kentish ragstone with a broach spire that makes an effective landmark. Near the church a small square is overlooked by the Black Horse pub, whose arched, white-painted windows were considered to be lucky by Sir Edward Cholmeley Dering, a local squire who had every house in Pluckley adapted to this design in the 19th century.

WALK 23
Tenterden (Wittersham Road) –
Small Hythe – Tenterden

Distance	5.5 miles/9km
Map	OS Explorer 125 'Romney Marsh, Rye & Winchelsea' 1:25,000
Start	Wittersham Road Railway Station (K&ES Railway) (grid ref 866287)
Access	By Kent & East Sussex Railway from Tenterden Town Tenterden is reached by bus from Ashford, Hastings, Maidstone, Tunbridge Wells and Rye
Parking	At Tenterden Town Railway Station (grid ref 862335)
Refreshments	None on walk, but pubs and cafés in Tenterden

Travelling by vintage steam train to get to the start of the walk adds a special quality to this outing. Run by a team of enthusiasts, the Kent & East Sussex Railway provides a limited service between Tenterden Town and Bodiam in East Sussex. Leaving the train at Wittersham Road, the walk begins among low-lying farmland that once formed part of the seabed between Small Hythe (south of Tenterden) and the Isle of Oxney on Romney Marsh. It then rises among vineyards, and goes through a valley with a man-made lake and woodland flush with wild flowers, before heading across open fields to Tenterden.

Note The Kent & East Sussex Railway operates a limited service throughout the year except November. For details ☎ 0870 606074 (office hours), or 01580 762943 (24hr talking timetable); **www.kesr.org.uk**

Buy a one-way ticket to Wittersham Road Station, a journey which takes about 20 minutes. On leaving the station bear left, go over the level crossing and follow the country road south for about 250m. Opposite Maytham Farm take a footpath on the left which strikes across two fields linked by a footbridge. Cross a second footbridge and turn left along the edge of a field, then maintain direction between trees and bushes to reach a substantial bridge spanning the Newmill Channel, a major tributary of the River Rother.

Over the bridge bear right to a pumping station, and continue round the edge of a large open field on the bank of the unfortunately named Reading Sewer, a substantial watercourse with which you keep company for some time. Pass a corrugated building and enter another field, still keeping alongside the watercourse. Ignore the bridge which carries a track across Reading Sewer to the B2082 road, and maintain direction until you draw level with a line of willows, at which point bear left and cross the field to the left-hand end of the trees. Here you enter a new field and walk ahead along its right-hand boundary beside a ditch.

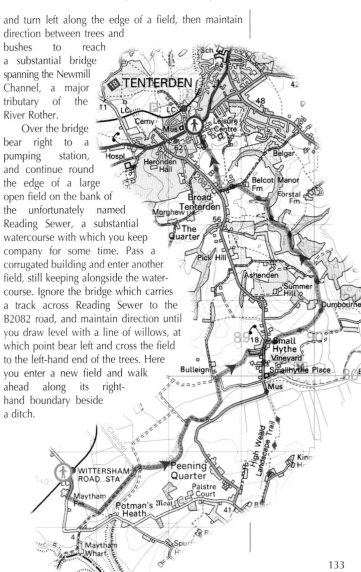

133

Below Small Hythe this drainage channel is raucous with Marsh frogs in springtime

In the field corner go over a stile, cross a drive near a red-brick, tile-hung house, and enter the field opposite. Bear half-right across this, making towards a collection of farm buildings seen several fields away. A plank footbridge takes you into a second field where you walk across to its far left-hand corner to find another stile. This leads onto a track that winds between vineyards and on to Spots Farm. Veer right alongside farm buildings, and follow a farm track/drive round to the B2082 at Small Hythe, which you reach through the vineyard car park at grid ref 894304.

Tenterden Vineyard at Spots Farm, Small Hythe, is the home of 'New Wave Vines' – guided tours of the vineyard and winery are available (☎ 01580 763033). About 150m south of the vineyard **Smallhythe Place** was the one-time home of Victorian actress Ellen Terry. Owned by the National Trust, the house and gardens are open to the public (☎ 01580 762334). The 16th-century house was originally built for the harbourmaster, in the days when Small Hythe was an important shipbuilding port.

134

Turn left along the road for about 100m, then through a gate by a telephone kiosk, cross a drive and keep along the right-hand side of a cypress hedge, now following the route of the High Weald Landscape Trail. At the bottom of the garden a stile takes you into a meadow where you continue ahead. A pair of oasthouses can be seen several fields away, and the walk will eventually pass close to them. In the bottom left-hand corner of the meadow go through a gateway and across another small meadow to a field gate and a stile in the far corner. Bear right round the edge of a sloping meadow and into the next meadow ahead where you continue along the right-hand boundary.

A stile and a footbridge near the bottom right-hand corner take you into the next field where you head towards the right of the oasthouses. Through a gate enter a small field below the oasthouse garden, cross another stile, then veer half-left then right, to walk along the left-hand boundary of a field which takes you through a gentle valley whose walling hills rise to woodland.

Woodland below Tenterden

135

At the far corner cross yet another stile and go ahead over a track to a stile and a footbridge over a brook whose banks are patched with wild garlic. Follow the brook ahead, and on reaching a grass-covered embankment, go up some steps to overlook a lake. Wander along its left bank; a delightful interlude. In springtime the banks are loud with the croaking of frogs advertising for mates.

Beyond the lake the path accompanies a stream running alongside a wood. Several stiles are crossed, then the way veers left through a narrowing of the valley, and enters the woodland which has a magnificent drift of bluebell and wild garlic (ramsons) in springtime. Keeping the stream to your left, ignore the first footbridge, but cross to the left bank at the second opportunity, then recross to the right bank shortly after. The path then goes up a slope and emerges into a meadow where you turn left. After about 150m bear right to a group of trees enclosing a pond. Go along the left-hand side of these to a stile, over which you bear half-left across a meadow, passing alongside a pond near Belcot Farm. In the top right-hand corner of the meadow come onto the farm drive and turn left.

Walk along the drive until it meets the B2082 road, where you then go through a gate on the right and follow a tarmac path all the way to Tenterden, where you arrive in the High Street opposite the parish church. Turn left, then right down Station Road to arrive once again at Tenterden Town Station.

WALK 24
Appledore – Stone-in-Oxney – Royal Military Canal – Appledore

Distance	7.5 miles/12km
Map	OS Explorer 125 'Romney Marsh' 1:25,000
Start	Court Lodge Road, Appledore (grid ref 956293)
Access	Via B2080 about 6 miles/9.5km southeast of Tenterden
	By train on the Ashford–Hastings line
	By bus from Tenterden
Parking	Free car park behind the village hall at north end of Appledore's main street
Refreshments	Pubs at Appledore, the Ferry Inn, and Stone-in-Oxney. Tearoom in Appledore.

Overlooking Romney Marsh, much of this route wanders through land reclaimed from the sea between 'high' promontories on which stand Appledore and Stone-in-Oxney. It's a fascinating corner of the county in which only a little imagination is needed to conjure up the sea-washed landscape of the past. Both the grassy Mill Mound outside Appledore, and gorse-lined Stone Cliff south of Stone, offer clear evidence that these were once sea cliffs, from which you gaze into low-lying farmland sliced with drainage channels. The Reading Sewer and River Rother are remnants of one-time estuarine waterways that made Oxney an island and Appledore a precarious peninsular. The walk also passes a former ferry and returns alongside the Royal Military Canal, created in the early 19th century as a means of blocking a possible Napoleonic invasion.

At the southern end of Appledore's wide main street opposite the church, walk down Court Lodge Road. Shortly after passing the entrance to Court Lodge, a second drive breaks left to Court Barn, where a stile gives access to a meadow. Following the route of the Saxon Shore Way, go onto an obvious hillock (Mill Mound)

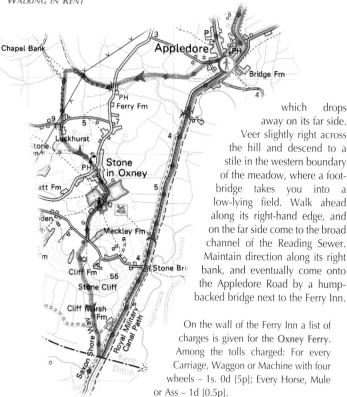

which drops away on its far side. Veer slightly right across the hill and descend to a stile in the western boundary of the meadow, where a footbridge takes you into a low-lying field. Walk ahead along its right-hand edge, and on the far side come to the broad channel of the Reading Sewer. Maintain direction along its right bank, and eventually come onto the Appledore Road by a humpbacked bridge next to the Ferry Inn.

On the wall of the Ferry Inn a list of charges is given for the **Oxney Ferry**. Among the tolls charged: For every Carriage, Waggon or Machine with four wheels – 1s. 0d [5p]; Every Horse, Mule or Ass – 1d [0.5p].

Cross the bridge, turn right opposite the pub to walk through its car park, and continue ahead along a bridleway with the Reading Sewer now on the right. On reaching a small pumping station, veer left alongside a minor drainage channel. This leads to a crossing farm road beside a bridge. Over the bridge wander south along the road until, shortly before it reaches a farm building, you take a footpath running parallel with the road in the right-hand field. Cross a stile and maintain direction through a small meadow to a second stile, which brings you onto a road at grid ref 935284.

Luckhurst, seen across its pond on the outskirts of Stone

On the south side of the road walk up the drive of a house named Luckhurst, but leave it when it curves left, then over a stile walk ahead among trees. Passing a neat pond on the left, bear left over a plank footbridge into a field. The right of way angles across this field to a point midway along its far right-hand boundary, but during research it appeared that most walkers cut round its right-hand boundary, first alongside the little woodland, then left at the field corner. Now with the boundary hedge on your right, keep ahead as far as a gap in the far corner, where you cross a ditch into the next field ahead. A Saxon Shore Way marker on a post directs you slightly right across this field to a gap in the far hedge. This brings you out at a junction of roads opposite the Crown Inn in Stone-in-Oxney at grid ref 939278.

Cross to the road cutting left of the pub, and follow it between houses, past the old church of St Mary and the timber-framed Tilmenden Hall next to it, and continue up Church Hill to gain wide views across Romney Marsh. At a T-junction cross to a stile just left of the driveway to a fine house named Tighe. Now walk along the right-hand edge of a meadow to another stile in the far boundary. Over this you go half-left across a sloping meadow overlooking a chequerboard of fields spreading into Sussex, with the high land beyond and to the right showing the borders of the one-time Rother Estuary.

139

In times past the Rother's estuary was a major waterway; now it's low-lying farmland

Below Coldharbour Farm cross yet another stile and maintain direction, sloping down and round Stone Cliff to a gate where you join a track. Curving below the gorse-fringed Stone Cliff come to another gateway. Through this leave the track and veer slightly right below a step of hillside, then cut down the slope to a stile in the bottom hedgerow. Cross the stile and a plank footbridge, then walk ahead alongside a minor drainage channel to reach a farm track. Follow this to a sharp bend by a small brick building, then break to the right on a path alongside another watercourse. Soon turn left at Kent Ditch, then right towards a bridge, over which you come onto the Military Road linking Appledore with Rye at grid ref 940252.

Cross the road with care and mount the grass and tree-lined embankment beside the Royal Military Canal. While the Saxon Shore Way heads to the right towards Rye, we turn left and follow the canal path for almost 3 miles/5km back to Appledore.

Shortly after joining the **Royal Military Canal** you come to an upright stone marking the county boundary, and just beyond this one of a series of oak posts indicating the distance between Hythe and Rye – 19 miles/30km along the canal path. The Royal Military Canal Path actually runs for a distance of 28 miles/45km between Seabrook near Hythe and Cliff End beyond Rye in East Sussex. For further information visit **www.royalmilitarycanal.com**

The Kent-Sussex boundary stone by the Royal Military Canal

NORTH AND EAST KENT

Dominated by the North Downs, but with an intricate coastline and secretive marshlands, North and East Kent also bears the brunt of the county's major transit routes, but it's worth reiterating that the walker sees a very different side of Kent from that experienced by the motorist, and there are huge swathes of countryside here where one may walk for hours at a stretch and see practically no one. While Rochester, Chatham, Canterbury and Dover have their crowded streets, there are walks included in this section that visit some of the most remote communities in southern England, and follow trails through landscapes of surprising isolation. Once again we discover that Kent is a county of extremes, with natural beauty being one of its prime features.

Chilham is one of Kent's most attractive villages (Walk 35)

WALK 25
Camer Country Park – Luddesdown – Great Buckland – Camer Country Park

Distance	6 miles/9.5km
Map	OS Explorer 148 'Maidstone & the Medway Towns' 1:25,000
Start	Camer Country Park, Meopham (grid ref 649670)
Access	Via minor road (signed) off A227 northeast of Meopham
	Nearest station: Sole Street (0.75 mile/1.25km)
Parking	Camer Country Park
Refreshments	None on route, but pubs at Lower Luddesdown and Meopham (both about 400m from the path); occasional refreshments at Camer Country Park

It seems hard to believe that Camer Country Park is less than 4.5 miles/7km from the heart of Gravesend as the crow flies, and Luddesdown a similar distance from Rochester, for this walk leads through some charming, peaceful countryside divorced from the world of commerce and industry in all save the distant march of electricity pylons. It's an ever-varied circuit on which the first half follows the route of the long-distance Wealdway, and it begins in an extremely popular and well-kept park. Established in 1971, Camer Country Park comprises some 45 acres/18 hectares of grassland and mature trees.

From the park entrance off Camer Park Road, walk directly ahead (the public toilets to your right) along the left-hand edge of the parkland, soon with the 18th-century Camer Court seen to the left. Leave the park at its far left-hand corner by a lodge, then turn sharp right on a track running alongside the park's boundary. This is the route of the Wealdway. Remain on the track when it veers away from the park, and follow it beyond a solitary house on the edge of Henley Wood. Continue along the left-hand side of the wood, then go through a gap in a hedge and walk along the left side of a field towards a pylon. The way continues through a strip of woodland, then you bear right in a field on Henley Down with Luddesdown church now seen in the valley below. Over a stile descend through scrub, then bear left along the top edge of a sloping field for about 150m, where you then take the first footpath on the right. This slopes downhill before rising to a narrow lane at grid ref 667663.

Cross the lane and ascend some steps into another field. Walk directly ahead to reach a boundary fence round Luddesdown Court, then turn left alongside this boundary. Cross a stile in the field corner, descend to a junction of lanes and turn right by Luddesdown church.

The Grade I listed manor of **Luddesdown Court** is said to have once been owned by Bishop Odo, William the Conqueror's half-brother, and is one of the oldest, continuously occupied houses in Britain. The church next door is mentioned in the

*Luddesdown,
secluded in the North
Downs*

Domesday Book; the tower and south porch date from the 14th century, but much of the remainder was rebuilt in 1866.

A private road goes ahead to Luddesdown Court, with a choice of paths by the gateway. Keep along the drive, passing between the church and a large, fanciful house. Just before the drive ends at a farmyard, cross a stile on the left and follow the path which now scores a straight line alongside a hedgerow, soon rising to gain fine views back onto Luddesdown. Enjoy this peaceful scene and reflect what might have been, had the Ministry of Defence had its way in the 1970s when it was proposed to turn this area into a tank training ground!

Near the head of the slope ignore the stile on the left, and continue uphill veering right to find another stile in the top boundary. Continue along the upper edge of a field above a valley known as the Bowling Alley. When the boundary cuts back to the right, wander across the field to a stile, then along the left-hand edge of the next field. A short distance along the boundary cross yet another stile and maintain direction through the next two fields. Eventually come onto a narrow road and turn right. In a few paces the road forks; take the right branch towards Great Buckland Farm.

Just beyond the farm leave the route of the Wealdway and go up some steps into a field. Cross two more stiles and head up the slope to the top left-hand corner to enter Rochester Forest, where a flight of timber-braced steps takes the way through the woodland. You then aim slightly left over a hilltop field, cross another stile in a fence and make for the far right-hand corner of a second field to join a narrow lane. Bear right and soon reach Coomb Hill Farm, a half-timbered 15th-century farmhouse with a large barn nearby. Keep ahead on a track between the farmhouse and the barn. In Dilmer Wood the track narrows to a footpath that slopes down-hill out of the wood, then crosses a meadow by a tennis court to gain a driveway near Dene Manor. Over the drive walk up a slope among trees and scrub to reach the very narrow Dene Road.

Cross to a track which soon provides views of Luddesdown once more. At the top of the slope join a stony track and continue ahead through Brimstone Wood and on to another narrow lane. Turn right, pass a farm in a dip, and about 300m after joining the lane turn left at a crossing path which takes you among trees at the bottom of a row of gardens. Eventually come to Foxendown Lane where you bear left for about 500m.

The lane makes a right-hand bend by Foxendown Farm. Immediately past a white house on the right take a narrow footpath into woods. Without leaving the woods turn right on a crossing path and soon come out to a field corner. Go through a nearby gap in the hedge and onto a clear path which cuts diagonally across a large open field. This brings you onto Camer Park Road where you bear left to regain the entrance to the Country Park.

WALK 26
Stansted – Fairseat – Hodsoll Street – Ridley – Stansted

Distance	5.5 miles/9km
Map	OS Explorer 148 'Maidstone & the Medway Towns' 1:25,000
Start	The Black Horse, Stansted (grid ref 606621)
Access	By minor road (signed) running east from A20 about 1 mile/1.5km southeast of West Kingsdown
	Stansted is served by infrequent Postbus from Gravesend
Parking	By the village playing field northwest of the war memorial junction, in Malt House Road
Refreshments	Pubs in Stansted and Hodsoll Street

Surprisingly peaceful hidden valleys scooped from the heart of the Downs provide the main landscape features of this walk. Isolated farms with the weight of centuries in their beams add architectural romance, and three small villages (in addition to Stansted) give a sense of community to a truly rural setting. The best is Hodsoll Street – neat flint cottages and a pub grouped around a triangular green; Ridley's church is almost absorbed within a neighbouring farmyard, and has an attractive thatched well-head nearby. Stansted itself is disjointed, with some of its houses perched on hills, while others stand beside a valley lane.

Note If you park by the village playing field walk across the field to its upper corner, then turn right and almost immediately left into Tumblefield Road to reach the start of the walk.

From The Black Horse wander up Tumblefield Road for about 200m, then turn left on a footpath by a small car park reserved for local residents. A stile gives access to a field, and another leads out of it on the far side to descend among scrub to a third stile. Bear half-right down a slope, then rise to the top far corner and enter Mingram Wood where a clear path winds through, then

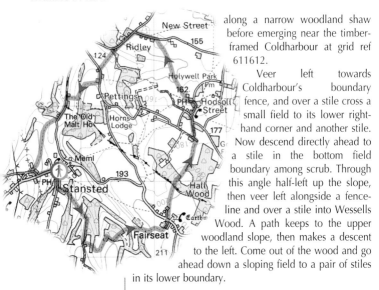

along a narrow woodland shaw before emerging near the timber-framed Coldharbour at grid ref 611612.

Veer left towards Coldharbour's boundary fence, and over a stile cross a small field to its lower right-hand corner and another stile. Now descend directly ahead to a stile in the bottom field boundary among scrub. Through this angle half-left up the slope, then veer left alongside a fence-line and over a stile into Wessells Wood. A path keeps to the upper woodland slope, then makes a descent to the left. Come out of the wood and go ahead down a sloping field to a pair of stiles in its lower boundary.

Wessells Wood near Stansted

The duckpond at Fairseat makes a colourful feature when the marsh marigolds are in flower

Now rise through three fields linked by stiles and field gates (fine views back to Stansted church), before veering left on the hilltop towards Court House Farm. A track, then drive, takes you through the farmyard and out to Vigo Road beside a tiny chapel at Fairseat (grid ref 622615). Cross to a swing-gate left of a duckpond, enter a field and aim for its far left-hand corner. Over a stile walk across another field to Westfield and Hall Woods. Once inside the woods take the right branch at a crossing path which leads among coppiced woodland, and when the way forks you take the left-hand option and soon emerge in the corner of an open field.

Walk along the right headland, and a short way along it veer right then left in a further section of woodland. This eventually leads to a bridleway enclosed by hedges that brings you onto a crossing track near farm buildings. Bear left into the farmyard, and about 20m later go through a gate on the right, then follow a track to the small village of Hodsoll Street. Walk ahead along a road, and at a junction maintain direction, soon to reach an attractive village green by The Green Man pub. A short distance beyond the pub bear left on a drive by Holywell Farmhouse. Passing between a shingle-hung cottage and some barns, enter a large field where you have a choice of paths – both of which lead to Ridley.

Take the right-hand option and cut across the field to its lower right-hand corner. Through a gate walk up the next slope angling towards the left-hand boundary where you will find a stile about two-thirds of the way up the slope. Over this the path continues across the highest part of a hilltop field which you leave by a stile just to the right of some farm buildings. Turn left along Bunker's Hill at grid ref 620639.

At a T-junction bear left to the few buildings of Ridley, passing between a thatched well-head and the church of St Peter. The road slopes downhill, and a very short distance after passing a house on the left, you turn left on a bridleway among trees. About 100m later break away to the right where a path descends to a stile and a large open field. The path cuts right through this field aiming half-left towards the top corner, near which a gap in the hedge gives access to a lane nearly opposite Campbell's Cottage. Bear left up Haven Hill, rounding a bend at the top. Immediately after passing the driveway to a house on the right, take a fenced path which parallels the drive and then enters another large field.

The handsome thatched **Bowdler's Well** in Ridley dates from 1810. On the other side of the road there's a small black granary perched on staddle stones to protect its contents from rodents.

When the field boundary cuts back to the right walk
ahead through the field to a gap in the opposite hedge,
and through this turn right and walk downhill to a field
gate giving onto a country lane at grid ref 608632. Bear
left, soon to pass the very fine thatched, timber-framed
Old Malt House. Baker's Wood is on the right of the lane.
Just beyond it enter a field and go half-left up a slope
towards a crown of trees. Before reaching them veer leftwards on a line towards a tall radio mast. A series of stiles
then direct the way over several fenced paddocks, and
out to a country road near some stables. Bear left, and left
again at a junction, and wander back to Stansted church
near The Black Horse pub.

*The decorated well-
head at Ridley*

WALK 27
Trosley Country Park –
Coldrum Stones – Ryarsh – Trosley

Distance	6.5 miles/10.5km
Map	OS Explorer 148 'Maidstone & the Medway Towns' 1:25,000
Start	Trosley Country Park (grid ref 633610)
Access	South of A227 Wrotham to Meopham road, about 2 miles/3km northeast of Wrotham; the Country Park turning is signed
	By bus on the Sevenoaks to Bluewater service
Parking	Trosley Country Park (fee charged). **Note** The park closes at dusk
Refreshments	Tearoom at the Country Park Visitor Centre, pubs (off route) in Trottiscliffe and Ryarsh

Set among broadleaved woods close to the steep scarp slope of the North Downs, Trosley Country Park covers an area of 170 acres/68 hectares, with some of the county's broadest panoramas revealed from several fine vantage points. Within the Park there's plenty of car parking space, picnic areas, a Visitor Centre, tearoom and public toilets. Information boards and leaflets outline some of the walking possibilities, and several circular routes have been waymarked and colour-coded. The North Downs Way passes through the Country Park, and the Pilgrims Way skirts the foot of the slope.

This walk descends the scarp slope to the edge of Trottiscliffe village, traces fields to Trottiscliffe church and continues to a Neolithic burial site. The route then cuts across more fields and through woodland to Ryarsh, before heading north for a return to the Country Park. Although there are steep slopes to contend with at the start and end of the walk, and a few minor hills in between, the majority of the route is either flat or gently undulating. Views are splendid almost all the way.

Just below the Visitor Centre bear left on a broad crossing path used by the North Downs Way. After about 250m turn right at a marker post directing the Blue Walk down

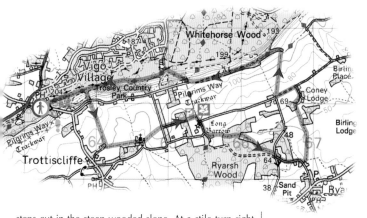

steps cut in the steep wooded slope. At a stile turn right beside a wire fence, and shortly after continue down the slope. On coming to a second wire fence bear left for about 200m where you then bear right between bars to cross the narrow lane of the Pilgrims Way into a meadow at grid ref 639610.

Walk down the right-hand boundary with Trottiscliffe church seen tucked in a hollow among farm buildings a couple of fields away. Eventually pass along the end of gardens and come to a crossing path. (For

Picturesque cottages by Trottiscliffe church

Trottiscliffe church

refreshments turn right into Trottiscliffe village where you'll find two pubs, The Plough and The George.) Turn left and wander ahead to the farmyard of Court Lodge Farm. A few paces beyond stands the flint-studded church of St Peter & St Paul.

> Dedicated to St Peter & St Paul, **Trottiscliffe church** is said to have been built on Saxon foundations by William the Conqueror's Bishop Gundulph in 1100. The tower was added 100 years later, and the church enlarged to its present size in 1270. Inside there are dark box pews and a pulpit that formally stood in Westminster Abbey.

Beyond the church pass an attractive 18th-century house and go up a footpath on the left. Halfway up the slope, pause to study the lovely group of church, houses and farm buildings below. The path continues through the centre of a large field, on the far side of which you come onto Pinesfield Lane opposite a row of bungalows. Take the narrow tarmac lane ahead which leads to a National Trust car park. From there go ahead on a track, and when this ends a footpath continues, goes along the edge of a field, then round to the right on a crossing track to pass below the Coldrum Stones at grid ref 655607.

The **Coldrum Stones**, or Coldrum Long Barrow, is an important Neolithic site in the care of the National Trust. Created some 4000–5000 years ago, the long barrow (burial chamber) originally consisted of 24 upright sarsen stones set in a rough circle measuring 160ft/48m in circumference, then covered with earth, with only the entrance kept clear. Only four of the stones are left standing, the remainder lie on the turf mound nearby. When the site was excavated in 1912, the skeletons of 22 humans and the remains of various animals were found.

Beyond the long barrow continue along a concrete farm road for a short distance until it curves to the right, where you leave it to go ahead on a track used by the Wealdway. At a crossing path turn left to find a pair of stiles. Cross the left-hand stile (thus leaving the Wealdway) into a field. When the field boundary cuts back to the left, maintain direction towards Ryarsh Wood. The woodland is divided into several sections, but as the path works its way through beware that in places it can be somewhat brambly.

Remains of a Neolithic burial chamber, the Coldrum Stones stand at the foot of the North Downs

The second woodland area leads to a third, and when you leave this you come onto a country lane opposite some cottages at grid ref 665604. Bear right, then almost immediately turn left down Chapel Street, which you follow for about 500m towards the village of Ryarsh, seen ahead with the M20 motorway behind it. When the lane curves to the right between houses, pass the first house on the left, then bear left along the edge of gardens. (For refreshments continue down the lane a short distance to The Duke of Wellington pub in Ryarsh village.)

The path swings left into fields where you then walk towards the North Downs, soon with a little brook for company – although this is often dry in summer. Go alongside a woodland, then on the right-hand edge of a field to a second woodland where the path bears right, then left through a gap, and right again to farm buildings and a concrete farm road. Turn left and wander on to the red-brick Coney Lodge Farm, set at a T-junction of farm roads at grid ref 667613.

Bear left again and continue towards Park Farm, but on reaching a barn turn immediately to the right where an enclosed bridleway heads towards the North Downs. (An alternative footpath cuts through the left-hand field and rejoins our route on the Pilgrims Way.) The bridleway becomes a narrow sunken track leading directly to a major crossing track, adopted here by both the Pilgrims Way and North Downs Way. Bear left for a little under 1 mile/1.5km, when the track becomes a narrow metalled lane.

Now turn right between houses and climb the steep scarp slope among dark yew trees. Near the head of the slope bear sharp left, go through a gate and re-enter Trosley Country Park. Simply follow the main trail ahead which leads all the way to the car park and Visitor Centre.

WALK 28
Newington – Upchurch – Lower Halstow – Newington

Distance	7 miles/11km
Map	OS Explorer 148 'Maidstone & the Medway Towns' 1:25,000
Start	Newington High Street (grid ref 859648)
Access	Via train on the London Victoria to Sittingbourne line (nearest station: Newington)
	By road on A2 about 4 miles/6.5km east of Gillingham
	Newington is served by bus from Chatham and Sittingbourne
Parking	Public car park by Newington Village Hall (grid ref 861648)
Refreshments	Pubs in Newington, Upchurch and Lower Halstow

From a start in Newington, on the A2 between Gillingham and Sittingbourne, this walk visits two other villages with fine churches, and traces part of the Saxon Shore Way alongside saltings of the Medway Estuary. It's an undemanding circular walk with lots of variety and interest.

At the western end of Newington High Street, opposite Playstool Road, a public footpath cuts between a house and a bungalow, passes beneath the railway line and enters a large open field. Walk across this aiming half-left, gently rising over the insignificant Mill Hill to gain a view of the Medway Estuary ahead. Come to a narrow lane, and over a stile maintain direction through linking fields and into the top edge of an orchard. After a few paces enter a field, then turn right round the outer boundary of the orchard, then left (still with the orchard on your right), and right again at the next boundary corner. After about 25m cross a stile on your left, and walk through linking fields to pass below a pylon. A stile next to a field gate brings you out to a minor crossroads at Boxted (grid ref 851663).

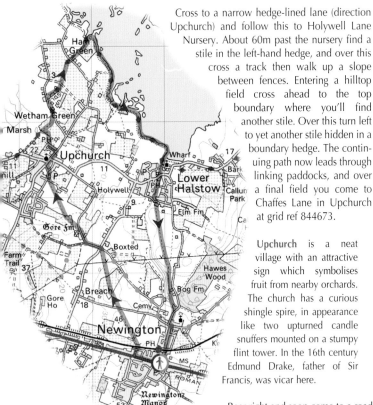

Cross to a narrow hedge-lined lane (direction Upchurch) and follow this to Holywell Lane Nursery. About 60m past the nursery find a stile in the left-hand hedge, and over this cross a track then walk up a slope between fences. Entering a hilltop field cross ahead to the top boundary where you'll find another stile. Over this turn left to yet another stile hidden in a boundary hedge. The continuing path now leads through linking paddocks, and over a final field you come to Chaffes Lane in Upchurch at grid ref 844673.

Upchurch is a neat village with an attractive sign which symbolises fruit from nearby orchards. The church has a curious shingle spire, in appearance like two upturned candle snuffers mounted on a stumpy flint tower. In the 16th century Edmund Drake, father of Sir Francis, was vicar here.

Bear right and soon come to a road junction where you again bear right, passing the church of St Mary the Virgin to your left. Continue ahead along The Street, and just before leaving the village turn left along a residential street named The Poles. When this curves left, take a footpath between houses, then half-left across a small meadow. Over a stile the narrow path is now funnelled between trees, at the end of which you come to the route of the Saxon Shore Way, with its waymark symbol of a Viking helmet. Turn right through another meadow to reach a lane at Wetham Green.

Beginning in Gravesend, the **Saxon Shore Way** traces the coastline as it was about 1500 years ago, as far as Hastings – a distance of 163 miles/262km (see Walk 49). Along this ancient coastline a series of fortifications were built to protect this part of southeast England from Saxon raiding parties. Several other walks in this book adopt sections of the SSW.

Turn left along the lane, and after about 250m come to a pair of bungalows on the left. Opposite these the Saxon Shore Way goes alongside a fence, passes riding stables, cuts across the top corner of a paddock, and then becomes an enclosed path. Coming to orchards walk along the left-hand edge, and when you reach a dividing hedgeline between more orchards, go along its left-hand side to reach another lane opposite Ham Green Farm. Turn right, then left after a few paces into the very narrow Shoregate Lane. When this ends bear right on a footpath which brings you alongside Hamgreen Saltings in the Medway Estuary at grid ref 849692.

The path now edges the saltings for 1.5 miles/2.5km as far as Lower Halstow. It's a pleasant section with views across the water to the Hoo Peninsular (the chimney

The path edges the Medway Estuary between Ham Green and Lower Halstow

The embankment path approaches Lower Halstow

belongs to Kingsnorth Power Station), to the spit of land of Chetney Marshes, and across Halstow Creek to Barksore Marshes. Inland are a few orchards and low-lying meadows; in the water small boats and the blackened, half-submerged skeletons of boats long-forgotten. The path skirts well to the left of Callows House, edges Twinney Wharf, and is most attractive just before reaching Lower Halstow.

The old Saxon **church of St Margaret of Antioch** in Lower Halstow is a gem of a building, standing on the edge of the Medway's marshlands. Inside a small 12th-century lead font is decorated with arches, kings and angels. Apparently the lead-work had been covered with plaster during the Civil War to prevent it being plundered to make bullets, but thanks to vibration caused by a battery of guns sited nearby during World War I, the plaster fell away to reveal the treasure it had been hiding. Sadly, like so many country churches, this one is kept locked except for service times.

The path turns towards Lower Halstow alongside an inlet – the church is on the opposite bank, reached by a causeway. Leaving the Saxon Shore Way walk into the village through a small residential area, and come onto the main road with the Three Tuns pub off to the left. Keep ahead along Burntwick Drive, another residential street. Near the end turn left on a path between houses, cross a small stream, then right on a concrete path leading to a crossing lane. Bear left, and in a few paces turn right alongside barns or stables. At the end of these the path goes through two small paddocks, then maintains direction across a large open field.

Just beyond a pylon go over a stile into a sloping meadow. Wander across the slope to the top end of a line of trees, then maintain direction to the bottom corner of the meadow where you'll find a stile among trees. The continuing path is a little rough as it picks a way over rabbit burrows among trees and scrub, edges along the garden boundary of a house, then crosses two footbridges into a final meadow notable for its inlet or water course. The way then goes alongside a fence and onto Wardwell Lane not far from Newington church. Turn right and soon come to a crossroads. Go ahead into Church Lane which leads to Newington High Street.

At the entrance to Newington's handsome flint-walled Norman church stands the **Devil's Stone**, a sarsen stone brought here by glaciers in the last Ice Age.

WALK 29
Leysdown-on-Sea – Shellness – Harty – Leysdown-on-Sea

Distance	7 miles/11km
Map	OS Explorer 149 'Sittingbourne & Faversham' 1:25,000
Start	Leysdown Country & Coastal Park (grid ref 045698)
Access	By bus from Sheerness
	By road, Leysdown-on-Sea is approached along B2231, east of Queenborough; the Country Park is located southeast of the village, along Shellness Road
Parking	Public car park at the Country & Coastal Park
Refreshments	None en route, but pub in Harty (+1km). Leysdown has pubs and cafès
Information	Tourism Section, Swale Borough Council ☎ 01795 417478, tourism@swale.gov.uk

The southeast corner of the Isle of Sheppey is a land of low-lying salt-marsh and meadow, edged in the east by Whitstable Bay and in the south by the Swale. With no hills to reduce the horizon, big skies are a feature. So is the birdlife, for thousands of wildfowl gather here – especially in winter. A short diversion from the main circuit of this walk gives an opportunity to visit the tiny church of St Thomas at Harty, the most remote in all Kent.

From the car park along Shellness Road go up onto the grass-covered sea wall and with Whitstable Bay on your left wander along the embankment. Should you choose to walk along the shoreline, rather than the embankment path, as far as Shellness hamlet, note that the cottages there form part of a private estate with no public access. You will have to backtrack on a footpath which runs inland behind and below the cottages to reach the Shell Ness Nature Reserve car park from where the walk continues.

Between a row of beach huts and the hamlet of Shellness itself lies the **Swale Naturist Beach**.

For the main walk, the path joins a track running just below the embankment, which you follow to its end at a small unmade car park for the Shell Ness National Nature Reserve.

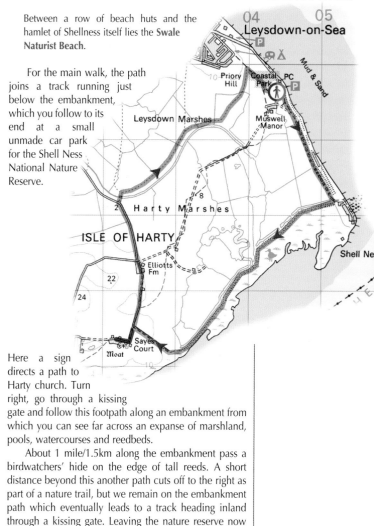

Here a sign directs a path to Harty church. Turn right, go through a kissing gate and follow this footpath along an embankment from which you can see far across an expanse of marshland, pools, watercourses and reedbeds.

About 1 mile/1.5km along the embankment pass a birdwatchers' hide on the edge of tall reeds. A short distance beyond this another path cuts off to the right as part of a nature trail, but we remain on the embankment path which eventually leads to a track heading inland through a kissing gate. Leaving the nature reserve now follow the tree-lined track to a signed junction at grid ref 024665. The main circular walk heads to the right here,

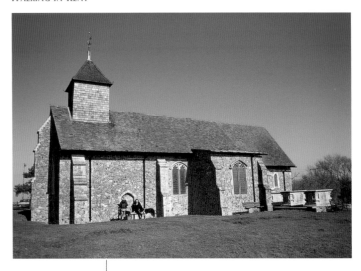

The church of St Thomas at Harty is the most remote in all Kent

but a brief diversion to Harty church is recommended.

For Harty church turn left and very soon you will come to the few buildings of the tiny hamlet, with the charming little church of St Thomas the Apostle overlooking the Swale. Return to the junction of tracks and continue ahead towards Elliotts Farm on a track lined by trees and scrub. After passing a solitary house walk ahead on a concrete farm drive which takes you through Elliotts Farm and on to Harty Ferry Road. Keep ahead with Harty Marshes on your right.

> Despite its remoteness the 900-year-old early Norman **church of St Thomas** is still used for monthly worship. Lit by the watery light of the Swale, and by oil lamps and candles, it gives a wonderful sense of peace. A short distance to the southwest, and reached by footpath from nearby Sayes Court, the historic Ferry House Inn is a reminder that there used to be a ferry link with Faversham across the Swale – see Walk 30 which passes the site of the mainland side of this ferry.

When the road curves left, note the raised Raptor Viewing Point on your right. Go through a gate just beyond this and along a track for about 120m, then turn right by a small fence-enclosed pumping station to follow a watercourse heading northeast for a little over 1 mile/1.5km.

The watercourse curves in a right-hand bow; as it does, about 100m before coming to a fence with a double gate, bear half-left and cross to a footbridge spanning a ditch. Over the bridge walk directly ahead up a field to a fence corner, then maintain direction with the fence to your left. On the far side of the field go through a metal kissing gate and turn right along a grass track with views of Whitstable Bay and a wind farm out at sea. You have now entered Leysdown Country & Coastal Park, and will shortly see the car park on the left where the walk began.

Harty Marshes on the Isle of Sheppey

WALK 30
Faversham – Oare Creek – Uplees – Oare – Faversham

Distance	6.5 miles/10.5km
Map	OS Explorer 149 'Sittingbourne & Faversham' 1:25,000
Start	The Guildhall, Faversham Market Place (grid ref 015615)
Access	By train on the London Victoria to Canterbury or Ramsgate lines
	By road, Faversham is reached by either the A2, or M2 motorway
Parking	Pay & display car park a short distance from the Market Place
Refreshments	Pubs and cafes in Faversham, pubs in Oare

From the heart of one of Kent's most handsome towns, to the solitude of marshland alongside the Swale, this walk has many attractive features. Stonebridge Pond at Davington is one, the boating haven of Oare Creek is another. There's plenty of birdlife, a gentle agricultural landscape to wander through, and always something of interest to gaze upon in the Swale. The walk itself is gentle and undemanding, but no less worthwhile for all that.

Leave the Market Place with its attractive Guildhall building, and walk along West Street which is soon crossed by South Road/North Lane. Remain along West Street between lovely old buildings, and when it ends

Stonebridge Pond, Faversham

turn right, shortly after which you come to Stonebridge Pond – this is always busy with duck, moorhen and coot. Immediately after the pond turn right to walk up Davington Hill, and curve left at the top of the hill to pass Davington's parish church at the entrance to Priory Road.

Faversham has no less than 450 listed buildings; a number of which are seen in the early stage of the walk. Standing on pillars, the **Guildhall** is one of the more obvious. Dating from 1574 this is located at the junction of three of the town's oldest streets, with a brightly painted Victorian pump next to it.

Walk along Priory Road, but a few paces after it curves left, turn right on a signed footpath next to a bungalow. This becomes an enclosed path running along the back of gardens and houses, with a lake seen beyond a fence on the right. At the end of the lake the path turns sharply to the right and is led by security fences past a complex of warehouses, and eventually brings you onto Oare Road where you turn left.

At the junction with the B2045, look to the right along Oare Creek. Between the Creek and The Castle pub, turn right onto a footpath cutting across a field, now on the route of the Saxon Shore Way. Through a kissing gate go up onto a raised embankment alongside the Creek, which you wander along for the next 1.5 miles/2.5km until the waterway opens into the Swale.

167

Oare Creek is an inlet of the Swale

The Swale is that stretch of tidal water that separates mainland Kent from the Isle of Sheppey. Flanked by grazing marshland, and with mudbanks exposed at low water, it attracts a huge concentration of wildfowl. Several nature reserves and specific bird reserves have been established on both the mainland and the Sheppey side.

The path enters Oare Marshes Nature Reserve which is now in the care of the Kent Wildlife Trust. On reaching the site of the long-abandoned Harty Ferry, note that just below the embankment there's a small building which houses the Oare Marsh Information Centre. The jetty here was formerly used by the ferry that served Harty, on the Isle of Sheppey to the north. Across the water, The Ferry Inn is less than a mile away (see Walk 29). Without the ferry, it's almost 30 miles/48km distant by road!

Keep on the raised path for another 0.5 mile/800m where you come to a few remains of another jetty and the way curves left, then forks. Turning your back to the Swale, go through a gate on the left and walk along a farm track between the marshes with their long, straight drainage ditches. The track leads to Gate House Bungalows, and continues as a stony drive.

When you reach a narrow crossing road at Uplees (grid ref 999645), keep ahead through a gate and walk along the left-hand edge of an old orchard, on the far side of which a stile gives onto a continuing fence-enclosed path. After about 80m turn left onto a crossing track. When this curves left, cross a stile on the right next to a field gate, and walk through a field along a line of electricity poles. The second of these poles is by the field boundary where you cross another stile and bear half-right.

Passing beneath high-voltage power lines come to a narrow country lane and turn right. After about 60m enter a field on the left and follow another line of electricity poles across a section of open field to a dividing fence and line of trees. Maintain direction beside these, and on reaching the top boundary enter the next field ahead and bear half-right, and you'll soon reach Uplees Road.

Turn left and follow this country lane into the village of Oare, then walk ahead along The Street which leads to The Three Mariners pub. Turn right into Mount Pleasant which shortly becomes a tarmac path. Go through a kissing gate into Oare Meadow Nature Reserve. A second kissing gate takes you out on the far side, where you then pass between a bungalow on the left and the white weatherboarded Grove Cottage on the right. Follow a stony drive ahead beside a long pond and come onto the B2045 road where you bear right. In a few paces cross the road and take a fence-enclosed tarmac path between warehouses. When you come to a crossing path turn right. Having now rejoined the outward path near Davington, retrace your footsteps back to Faversham.

WALK 31
Faversham – Ham Marshes –
Oare Creek – Faversham

Distance	5 miles/8km
Map	OS Explorer 149 'Sittingbourne & Faversham' 1:25,000
Start	The Guildhall, Faversham Market Place (grid ref 015615)
Access	By train on the London Victoria to Canterbury or Ramsgate lines
	By road, Faversham is reached by either the A2, or M2 motorway
Parking	Pay & display car park a short distance from the Market Place
Refreshments	Pubs and cafes in Faversham, pub on Ham Marshes.

Making a circuit of Ham Marshes due north of Faversham, this gentle, level walk spends most of its journey either beside Faversham Creek or Oare Creek, and if the tide is right, there will probably be added boating interest.

From the Guildhall walk through the pedestrianised Market Place and along Court Street, soon passing the Shepherd Neame building on the left at number 17, its doorway decorated with hops. About 100m past this turn left into Quay Lane, which curves left by the Swan and Harlequin pub. As you walk along here note the fine old timber building used by Faversham Sea Cadets, then turn right into Bridge Road.

Cross Faversham Creek and turn right alongside Front Brents, a service road used by the Saxon Shore Way, which soon takes you past the tiny Albion pub. A footpath continues ahead through a meadow, curves left round the edge of a housing development, then the outer edge of an industrial unit. Coming into meadowland turn right at a path junction and return to Faversham Creek. Bear left on the raised grass embankment, still on the Saxon Shore Way.

Faversham was once a flourishing port, and in 1225 the town gained the status of a 'limb' of the Cinque Port of Dover. During the Middle Ages Faversham Creek was an important waterway, busy with sailing barges bringing cargoes of timber and other raw materials for local industries, and shipping out hay and bricks by return; a trade that continued until the 1930s.

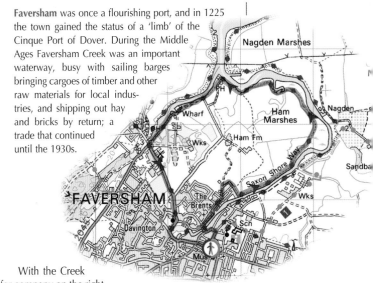

With the Creek for company on the right, and low-lying sheep-grazed grassland on the left, the way heads northeastward with the seemingly remote Nagden Cottages seen ahead on the opposite bank of the Creek. The embankment path curves left, with Nagden Marshes stretching beyond the waterway out towards Whitstable Bay.

Eventually come to The Shipwright's Arms at the confluence of Faversham and Oare Creeks. Leaving the pub below on the left, the path takes you past a small boatyard and alongside Oare Creek, now heading southwest. For much of the walk round Ham Marshes, birdlife has been fairly prominent, but hereon boats dominate. Diverting slightly away from Oare Creek the path eases among bushes of dog roses extravagant with flowers in early summer.

Come onto a rough service road by a boatyard and wander ahead along it, now beside the Creek once more with the village of Oare seen on the far side. On reaching a roundabout on the B2045 turn left (The Castle pub is a

The walk follows Faversham Creek onto Ham Marshes

short distance away to the right), now leaving the route of the Saxon Shore Way. Before long note a black windmill on the left – minus its sails. Follow the road into Davington, and down the hill to Stonebridge Pond. Bear left at a T-junction to pass alongside the pond, and left again by The Bull Inn which takes you into West Street in Faversham. This leads directly to the Guildhall in the Market Place where the walk began.

WALK 32
Wye – Crundale – Coombe Manor – Wye

Distance	7 miles/11km
Map	OS Explorer 137 'Ashford, Headcorn, Chilham & Wye' 1:25,000
Start	Wye church (grid ref 054468)
Access	About 3 miles/4.5km northeast of Ashford, off A28 Nearest railway station, Wye
Parking	Public car park near the church
Refreshments	Pubs & shops in Wye

The Great Stour has forced a passage through the North Downs between Ashford and Canterbury. Wye is contained on its east bank, with the Downs rising as an impressive wall behind the town. This is splendid walking country; scenically dramatic and peaceful, with extensive views from the lip of the Downs, or from their folds that create a secretive heartland of isolated farms and half-forgotten hamlets; a land where larks fill the air with endless song. This outing explores one such hidden corner. There are tremendous views to enjoy, and wild flowers to study in the woods and on the open Downs (cowslip, orchid, bluebell, blood-red campion, yellow archangel, the deep blue of bugle, and ramson – wild garlic – by the acre in springtime). Birds will doubtless serenade you, while its possible that rabbit, fox, badger, or even deer will surprise you. Butterflies mass the summer grasslands, and from the secluded church-yard at Crundale you can wonder that such places still exist, here in the 'overcrowded southeast'.

Note To make a longer, 10-mile/16km circuit, it's possible to link this route with Walk 33 at point A on the map.

From the main street in Wye take the footpath branching half-right through the churchyard on the route of both the North Downs Way and Stour Valley Walk. Continue between allotments and the buildings of Wye Agricultural College. After the path bears right, cross a narrow road and maintain direction along a driveway heading towards the wall of the Downs.

Founded in 1432 by Cardinal John Kempe as a semi-nary college for priests, **Wye College** became a grammar school in the 16th century. In 1894 the buildings and grounds were adapted for use as an agricultural college, and in 1900 became a faculty of London University.

The drive becomes a track between fields, and as you progress along it you may notice a large memorial crown set in the chalk slope half-right ahead. On the return journey your path crosses above it.

Cross another narrow road, then keep ahead on a footpath which takes you through a gate, then steeply uphill among trees. At the head of the slope come onto a very narrow lane and turn right along it for about 450m. As you wander along the lane, the slope to the left plunges into a deep valley flowing to the north where another section of the Downs can be seen stretching blue into the distance. The lane swings left by a house on the crest of the hill. Leave it here and walk ahead on a track towards Collyerhill Wood, which you enter by a gate. Here the track swings left and traces the woodland edge with Down Farm

seen a short distance away. On emerging from the woods wander along the right-hand edge of a field.

Beyond the woods a line of oak trees stretches ahead, leading the path to a second woodland. Bear slightly left along its edge to reach an enclosed corner where a field gate gives access to a track easing gently downhill among trees, shade-loving flowers (wood anemone, violet and bluebell in springtime) and the unseen scrabbling of woodland creatures. It soon becomes apparent that you're descending a downland spur, with valleys stretching ahead on either side.

Out of the trees a path branches to the right, but you ignore this and follow the continuing track as it winds leftward, descending to a junction of tracks at grid ref 082476. Turn right alongside a wooded bank notable for a large number of hellebore growing within it, and soon come to a concrete farm road. Bear left for about 30m, then turn right and walk down the edge of a field towards Crundale Downs. At the bottom of the field bear left on a bridleway which slips into the right-hand field, where you then walk along its bottom boundary towards the hamlet of Crundale.

Edging the foot of the slope, with a view of houses ahead, the bridleway brings you to a path junction. Bear right and climb a steep slope, at the top of which you come onto a very narrow road. Turn right to reach Crundale church, which is certainly worth a visit. A few bench seats below the church make the most of the splendid views.

Dedicated to St Mary, the flint-towered **church at Crundale** dates from the early 13th century, on a site used by the Romans.

Take the bridleway that passes below and to the right of the church heading south, soon going along the narrow crest of Crundale Downs, with a lovely valley on either side, and with woodland ahead. This is an airy, peaceful section, with far-reaching views over a barely inhabited countryside. After walking alongside it for a

Coombe Manor nestles in a fold of the Downs

short distance, you then enter Town Wood which, once again, is magnificent with spring flowers. Eventually the bridleway slopes down to a crossing track where you go straight ahead into a field by way of a stile almost hidden among trees. (During research this stile had collapsed; hopefully it will soon be replaced.)

Walk along the right-hand edge of the field, and on the far side at a woodland corner bear left for a few paces before entering a second field alongside Hurst Wood. Maintain direction to the far corner where a stile directs the way through trees, then out to a slope with the farm buildings of Coombe Manor seen below. Descend towards them, but near the foot of the slope bear left round a fenced boundary to reach a farm access road just to the left of the manor at grid ref 080463. The complex of buildings, set among trees in a peaceful valley, makes an attractive scene.

Turn left along the road, and after about 120m you will reach the corner of a wood on the right. Follow round the boundary of the right-hand field alongside the woodland with views down to Coombe Manor. Drifts of wild garlic spread like snowfields in springtime, the heavy smell of the flowers almost overpowering, yet each bloom is full of delicate stars. At a field corner take the continuing path up the slope through the woods, to emerge into a hilltop field. Continue across this on a walk in the sky to a gate beyond which it seems as though the world falls away at your feet. It's an airy view of plunging downland and enormous vistas; the flat agricultural land far below, and blue hills in the distance. With larks overhead and flowers at your feet, this is a splendid place to sprawl in the grass and dream, for an hour – or so!

Note It is at this point (A on map) that you come onto the route of Walk 33, so if you want to make a longer return to Wye, turn left here and follow directions given for that walk.

Continuing on our route, bear right along the escarpment, now on the path of the North Downs Way, and

Wye Downs give a wonderful sense of space and far views

soon come to an undulating stretch with several small hollows. Nearby a stone seat has been provided at the Wye Crown Millenium Stone. Views, of course, are far-reaching over the expanse of the Weald.

> The **memorial crown** was cut in the chalk of the downs by students of Wye College to celebrate the coronation of Edward VII in 1902.

Continue ahead as far as woodland where you turn right, cross a stile and wander along the edge of a field to a narrow lane – recognisable from the outward route. On this bear left and retrace your steps to the woodland path that plunges steeply down the slope to open fields, beyond which you come into Wye.

WALK 33
Wye – Wye Downs – Cold Blow – Wye

Distance	5.5 miles/9km
Map	OS Explorer 137 'Ashford, Headcorn, Chilham & Wye' 1:25,000
Start	Wye church (grid ref 054468)
Access	About 3 miles/4.5km northeast of Ashford, off A28
	Nearest railway station: Wye
Parking	Public car park near the church
Refreshments	Pubs and shops in Wye

Not only does the Wye Downs escarpment provide magnificent views over the Stour Valley and distant Romney Marsh, the nature reserve visited on this walk protects as fine a chalk grassland as may be found anywhere in the county. Orchid, cowslip and butterfly adorn the slope; rabbits burrow in the scoops and hollows while skylark and kestrel hover overhead. Deer may also be seen in and on the edge of woodland. The North Downs Way makes a traverse of this glorious escarpment, and our route follows its path for some of the way, enjoying a vast panorama before descending the scarp slope for a return to Wye through low-lying fields and woodland shaws.

Enter Wye churchyard and take the path of the North Downs Way branching right through it. This continues beside allotments, then curves right, crosses a service road and maintains direction between Wye College buildings, eventually on a track heading towards the Downs. Over a minor crossing road continue ahead to a gate, through which a chalk path climbs the steep wooded slope and emerges onto a narrow lane. Turn right, and after about 300m when the woodland ends, go up steps on the right and walk ahead to the lip of the Downs. Cross a stile and turn left along the edge of the escarpment.

*Commemorative stone
on Wye Downs*

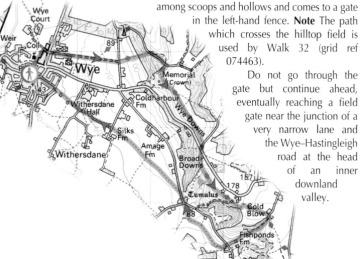

Very shortly you pass above the crown cut in the steep slope by Wye College students in 1902 to mark the coronation of Edward VII. After this the way weaves among scoops and hollows and comes to a gate in the left-hand fence. **Note** The path which crosses the hilltop field is used by Walk 32 (grid ref 074463).

Do not go through the gate but continue ahead, eventually reaching a field gate near the junction of a very narrow lane and the Wye–Hastingleigh road at the head of an inner downland valley.

Bear right on the lane and cross the road to enter the wooded section of Wye Downs National Nature Reserve at Pickersdane Scrubs. Emerging from the woods the way curves right, then leads over close-cropped open downland, once more with big panoramic views to the right.

> Established in 1961, **Wye Downs National Nature Reserve** covers 250 acres/101 hectares of downland on the steep face of the escarpment. Among its many wild flowers, 17 species of orchid have been recorded here. The dry valley known as the Devil's Kneadingtrough is a major feature of the slope.

Remain with the North Downs Way and you'll eventually come to a stile. Continue ahead with the woodland of Newgate Scrubs to the right, and a wire fence on the left. Led by a fence near kennels, the path curves left, then right, and enters a hilltop field. Follow the left-hand boundary to a field gate, and then a track near the barns of Cold Blow Farm at grid ref 086448. Here you leave the North Downs Way, turn right, and when the track forks in a few paces, go straight ahead on a bridleway, descending the slope among trees, and between banks of cowslips in springtime.

The Devil's Kneadingtrough is a dry valley within the Wye Downs National Nature Reserve

Seen from the lip of Wye Downs, Brook lies in a chequer-board landscape

At the foot of the slope cross the Pilgrims Way near Fishponds Farm, then go over a stile beside a barn and walk ahead to a second stile by a pond. Cross a brook to a third stile, then bear right through a field. A series of stiles linked by traces of footpath take you alongside the brook, then through trees to an open field. Follow the right-hand boundary until it cuts back, then maintain direction to a gate in the opposite boundary. The way then goes along the edge of a vineyard and into a field, on the far side of which go over a track and across towards a house at a junction of lanes (grid ref 074450).

The left-hand lane goes to Brook, but we go ahead along Amage Road which leads to Wye. After about 60m cross a stile on the left and walk across a field to its far corner. The footpath then continues along the boundary of several fields, passes Silks Farm and crosses its drive. Maintain direction on a track that leads to a narrow lane near Withersdane Hall – part of Wye Agricultural College. When the lane curves sharply to the left, continue ahead alongside a tall beech hedge to a narrow residential street. This leads to a crossing road where you bear left, and after a while turn right into Church Street which brings you to Wye parish church.

WALK 34
Chilham – Julliberrie Downs – Chilham

Distance	5 miles/8km
Map	OS Explorer 137 'Ashford, Headcorn, Chilham & Wye' 1:25,000
Start	The Square, Chilham (grid ref 068536)
Access	Via A28/A252 southwest of Canterbury
	By bus from Canterbury
Parking	Free public car park at entrance to village beside A252 (grid ref 066536)
Refreshments	Pubs and tearoom/restaurant in Chilham

Chilham is without question one of Kent's most attractive villages, with a Jacobean mansion (Chilham Castle), a handsome church, an almost perfect village square of half-timbered houses, and a street descending from each corner; some of these streets lined with yet more delightful half-timbered buildings. The village stands on a raised plot of land overlooking the Stour Valley, with the rolling Downs on either side, the Great Stour snaking below. This walk explores that landscape in a gentle, undemanding circuit.

Facing the castle gates in the village square, turn left and wander down School Hill alongside the wall surrounding the castle grounds, then at a junction of lanes bear right along Mountain Street. Towards the end of the wall a view opens to the right across a small lake to the Jacobean mansion. Continue along the lane after the wall ends, and just beyond the second house on the left, take a footpath which goes along the right-hand side of April Cottage.

Built on a promontory commanding the Stour Valley, 12th-century **Chilham Castle** was once described as being 'not only commodious for use but also strong

for defence and resistance'. However, much of that castle was demolished for building materials, although the keep remains, with the red-brick mansion close by completed in 1616 for Sir Dudley Digges, Master of the Rolls for James I.

Entering a field bear right, then cut straight across it to a stile in the far boundary, from which there is a good view of Chilham Castle to the north. Over the stile turn right along the edge of a meadow, and maintain direction in a second meadow. Towards the end of this second meadow a footpath sign directs you half-left across it to a bridge over the Great Stour at grid ref 074521. (**Note** This bridge is different from that marked on the OS map.) Over the bridge cross the A28 Ashford to Canterbury road and walk along the drive of East Stour Farm. With the farmhouse on your left go over a stile and pass beneath a railway bridge. About 30m beyond the bridge cross a stile on the left onto a path running between a fence and a row of old elder trees and scrub growing in a slope riddled with rabbit burrows.

Heading north along the slopes of Chilmans Down the path brings you to a farm track. Continue ahead, soon curving right above Julliberrie Downs to be joined by a path adopted by the Stour Valley Walk. Remain on the track to pass alongside, then through the lower edge of Long Wood, eventually arriving at the narrow Pickelden Lane at grid ref 093538.

Julliberrie Downs is the site of a Neolithic long barrow, and it was on land near here that the Romans are thought to have fought their last great battle against the Britons.

The path through Long Wood on Julliberrie Downs

Chilham Mill is seen near the end of the walk

Turn left, wander gently downhill, then bear left by Lake House. When the lane curves right by Pickelden Farmhouse, leave it to cross a stile beside a field gate directly ahead, then follow the right-hand field boundary. At the far corner enter the next meadow ahead and maintain direction along the upper edge of a brief slope towards Stile Farm. With an enclosed path taking you between a house and the farm, turn right along the farm drive. After a few paces enter a large field on the left and walk along its right-hand edge.

At the far end of the field go ahead for a few paces to a crossing footpath, where you then turn right to descend among trees with the Great Stour below and the tall white Chilham Mill on the opposite bank. Come to a drive and cross a bridge by the mill, which is owned by the Mid-Kent Water Company. Remain on the drive to a level crossing over which you arrive at the A28. Cross with care and continue ahead along Bagham Lane to a junction with the A252. Turn left, then walk up the minor road to arrive at the village square in Chilham.

WALK 35
Stodmarsh Nature Reserve –
Grove Ferry – Stodmarsh

Distance	4.5 miles/7km
Map	OS Explorer 150 'Canterbury & the Isle of Thanet' 1:25,000
Start	Stodmarsh National Nature Reserve car park (grid ref 221609)
Access	By minor road (Stodmarsh Road) off A257, 5 miles/8km north east of Canterbury
Parking	Stodmarsh Nature Reserve car park, reached by track from the Red Lion pub in Stodmarsh village
Refreshments	Pubs at Grove Ferry, and at Stodmarsh, 500m from walk

Downstream from Canterbury, and spreading south of the Great Stour towards the Isle of Thanet, an impressive region of reedbed, meadow, and watercourse attracts large flocks of wildfowl, and provides a refuge for water rail, bearded tit, reed bunting, marsh harrier and wintering bittern. (To check sightings, log onto the Kent Ornithological Society website: **www.kentos.org.uk**) It is said that Augustinian monks were responsible for flooding the low-lying meadows with river water, and the resulting marshland (Studmarsh) provided good grazing for their horses. But after colliery workings caused subsidence in the last century, the land became waterlogged, with reedbeds and lagoons appearing in the 1930s to create new habitats. Now protected as a National Nature Reserve of some 595 acres/241 hectares, this interesting and strangely attractive region is explored by the following circular walk on mostly well-defined and waymarked footpaths.

Leave the car park at its far left-hand corner just beyond the public toilets, on a broad footpath adopted by the Stour Valley Walk. When the path forks shortly after, with one going ahead signed to the Reedbed Hide, keep to the main path curving right, but at the next junction go straight ahead between watercourses. You're now on the raised bank of the Lampen Wall which takes you among reedbeds, lagoons and watercourses all the way to Grove Ferry. Pass the Lake Hide on your left, and before long the path becomes a riverside walk with the Great Stour on one side, tall reedbeds on the other.

> The **Lampen Wall** is a dyke built across the Wantsum marshes in the 17th century as a sea defence.

Below Port Farm (grid ref 225626) boats are often moored, adding colour to the scene. Here a path cuts to the right to Harrison's Drove Hide, while the main path continues alongside the Stour and eventually brings you onto a road by the Grove Ferry Inn. Walk ahead along the road for a few paces to a small lay-by, then turn right onto the return footpath. This takes you below a raised bank viewing area, once again among reedbeds.

As its name suggests, a ferry used to operate at **Grove Ferry** until it was replaced by a road bridge in 1960. Nearby riverside meadows were formerly used for growing lavender, and the prominent chimney adjacent to the inn marks the site of the old lavender distillery.

At a T-junction of paths turn right, then left through a kissing gate after a few paces. Entering a meadow the path is less well defined than those previously used, as you follow a minor watercourse then cut across the meadow to a footbridge. Ignore a second footbridge just beyond, to walk ahead between two narrow watercourses.

The way through Stodmarsh Nature Reserve
is shared with the Stour Valley Walk

The tiny village of Stodmarsh

Come to a crossing track, go through the kissing gate ahead and maintain direction. At the next junction by the Marsh Hide continue ahead to weave among reedbeds before reaching yet another path junction near Newborns Farm. Turn right and soon pass Undertrees Farm seen off to the left. At the next junction veer right, then left at a T-junction of paths where you rejoin the outward route. Follow this back to the car park.

WALK 36
St Nicholas at Wade – Chitty – Sarre – St Nicholas at Wade

Distance	6.5 miles/10.5km
Map	OS Explorer 150 'Canterbury & the Isle of Thanet' 1:25,000
Start	St Nicholas church, St Nicholas at Wade (grid ref: 265666)
Access	Near junction of A299/A28 about 6 miles/9.5km southwest of Margate
	By bus from Canterbury or Margate
Parking	With discretion in the village
Refreshments	Pubs in St Nicholas and Sarre

Much of this walk takes place on land that once was sea, for the River Wantsum that made Thanet an island cuts right through the Chislet and Sarre Marshes before joining the Great Stour south of the A253. Measuring about 1 mile/1.5km across, the tidal Wantsum Channel was a major shipping lane from Roman times on, being used as a short cut for vessels plying their trade between the Thames Estuary and the Continent, but in the Middle Ages the channel began to silt up, and now footpaths cross a flat landscape where once ships sailed. This farmland is criss-crossed with drainage channels, and there's also evidence of medieval saltworks, while the walk adopts a section of a one-time drove road used to move flocks of sheep across the marshland. Chitty hamlet and the village of Sarre were once linked by ferry, and both places have some charming old buildings, as does St Nicholas at Wade where the walk begins and ends.

From the large and impressive church of St Nicholas head northwest along Court Road, and on the outskirts of the village, not far from the A299, bear left along a lane signed to St Nicholas Court. This leads to a complex of farm buildings, and a few paces after passing a large Dutch barn you turn left along a farm drive between

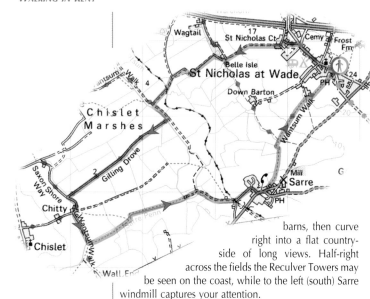

barns, then curve right into a flat countryside of long views. Half-right across the fields the Reculver Towers may be seen on the coast, while to the left (south) Sarre windmill captures your attention.

Come to the isolated white-painted cottage of Belle Isle at grid ref 252668, where the farm drive is crossed by the bridleway of the Wantsum Walk. Remain on the drive as it curves past the cottage along the right-hand side of the Wade Marsh Stream. The drive then veers left, with an embankment seen to the right containing a farm reservoir.

On reaching a bridge over the River Wantsum the concrete drive ends. Maintain direction on a grass track along the right-hand edge of a field, on the far side of which you come to a raised embankment by the Whitfield Sewer. Turn left along this embankment for about 350m, then cross the stream on a footbridge. The continuing footpath soon takes you between trees and bushes, then widens to a track known as Gilling Drove.

Eventually come to a very narrow lane, which you follow left to the few buildings of Chitty. Wander round the bend by The Old Schoolhouse, next to which stands Ferryman's Cottage, then turn left onto a track used by

Crossing the Whitfield Sewer, on land that once was sea

the Saxon Shore Way. This takes you through some trees, but on emerging from them the unusual tower of Chislet church can be seen off to the right. Crossing the watercourse of Sarre Penn, leave the Saxon Shore Way and bear left on the continuing track. (**Note** This track is not marked on the OS map, nor is the current route correctly shown, for there is no means of recrossing Sarre Penn southwest of the pumping station.) When the track curves to the right, leave it and maintain direction ahead on a grass embankment.

After passing a pumping station (on the opposite bank) the watercourse curves to the right, shortly after which you cross a footbridge onto a gravel track and follow this to the right. Cross a stile beside a field gate, then turn left along a narrow lane which brings you to Old Road beside the handsome Bolingbroke Farm in Sarre village. Turn right to pass several lovely old buildings, then bear left alongside the A28. At the village square, dominated by the King's Head Inn (an ale house since 1630) the road forks. Continue for a few paces along the A28 Margate road, then cut left at a gravel drive where a tree-lined footpath takes you above it, then out to a large open field. When the right-hand boundary hedge ends, an alternative path breaks to the right leading to Sarre windmill.

Easily reached by a short diversion, **Sarre Mill** is an attractive working windmill open to the public. There's also a museum, tearoom and gift shop.

Continue ahead across the field towards the right-hand end of a farm reservoir. The path is then enclosed by trees and scrub, and emerges to another large field. Maintain direction, rising gently towards St Nicholas at Wade. Pass a row of houses, walk alongside the village playing field, and arriving at The Street opposite the post office, turn left to the church where the walk began.

Sarre Windmill is open to the public

WALK 37
Bridge – Patrixbourne – Kingston – Bishopsbourne – Bridge

Distance	6.5 miles/10.5km
Map	OS Explorer 150 'Canterbury & the Isle of Thanet' 1:25,000
Start	Bridge High Street (grid ref 181545)
Access	By minor road signed from A2 southeast of Canterbury
	By bus from Canterbury
Parking	With discretion in the village
Refreshments	Pubs in Bridge, Kingston and Bishopsbourne

Southeast of Canterbury the valley of the Nailbourne stream is a delight of parkland and peaceful villages. This walk links three of these villages with a fourth, attractive Patrixbourne, which lies just to the north of the A2 and is visited by both the Elham Valley Way and the North Downs Way. Our walk briefly follows the North Downs Way out of Patrixbourne before striking away for a while through orchard country. Above Kingston the busy A2 has to be crossed, where extreme caution is essential. After that, a very pleasant return is made through the Nailbourne parklands.

At the top (Canterbury) end of Bridge High Street opposite the village post office, turn into the residential Conyngham Lane. At the far end take a bridleway on the right by the last house, then through a gate and a small field to pass beneath the A2. While the path of the Elham Valley Way goes to the right, we walk ahead alongside a fence to the far right-hand field corner. Cross a stile and turn right to a second stile which takes you into a park-like meadow. Leave this after about 200m by another stile in the right-hand fence, then along a drive to a junction of roads on the edge of Patrixbourne – note the Tudoresque chimney stacks at the lodge.

Turn right and walk down The Street through Patrixbourne to pass several attractive houses. The Street curves to the right passing St Mary's church, and twists left then right to leave the village. Now take the signed North Downs Way footpath round the large field on the left.

Wandering through Patrixbourne note the carved elephants at the gable end of a half-timbered cottage, and a pair of lions at the other end. Patrixbourne Oast has Dutch gables and a hoist wheel above the street by which loads would have been winched into the upper storey of the building. Spend a few minutes at the lovely church of St Mary (built about 1200) whose south doorway bears some remarkable carvings.

The way soon edges woodland, and about halfway along this you come to a bench seat at a path junction. Leave the North Downs Way here and take the bridleway through the woods. On emerging at the far side maintain direction along the edge of an orchard, at the end of which you keep ahead on a concrete farm road beside more orchards. When the road swings to the right towards Highland Court Farm, leave it and continue directly ahead along the lower edge of a field of fruit bushes. At the far side pass through a gap into the field ahead, then turn

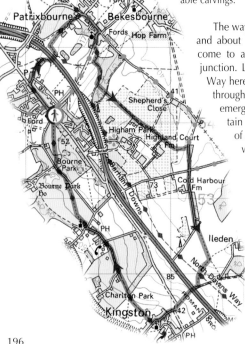

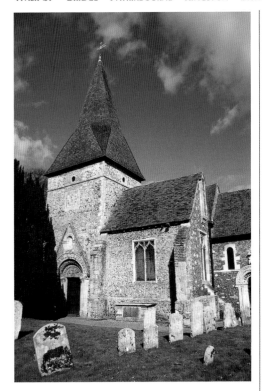

Patrixbourne's church was built around 1200

immediately to the left. At first following a line of trees the way is then enclosed by trees and hedges leading to a narrow lane at grid ref 203536.

Turn right and shortly come to crossroads. Keep ahead to pass above Coldharbour House, and when the lane bends to the right by the small white-painted Gypsy Cottage, cross a stile on the left to enter a very large field. A footpath strikes across this field making towards the far corner. About two thirds of the way across there's a line of well-spaced mature trees; a few paces beyond these turn right on a crossing path to a stile in the boundary fence. Over this angle slightly left ahead, and when you

197

begin to slope downhill, aim towards the bottom left-hand corner of the field where another stile gives access to the bottom of a lane by the busy A2 at grid ref 203518.

Cross the main road with great care, using the central reservation to wait for a gap in the traffic if necessary. Once across wander down the edge of a field with Kingston seen below. At a junction of lanes walk ahead into the village, crossing the Nailbourne stream as you do. Passing a few bungalows on the right-hand side of the street, a sign directs you onto a bridleway between the final two bungalows. This is heading for Bishopsbourne. After going through a gate the bridleway, adopted by the Elham Valley Way, is enclosed by fences.

The **Nailbourne** is an 'intermittent stream' – often being dry for several years at a stretch.

Shortly after the end of the fenced section, cross the Nailbourne again and enter the parkland of Charlton Park, an imposing Georgian mansion seen off to the left. Come onto the drive which leads into the small one-street village of Bishopsbourne; a pleasant row of cottages, the Mermaid Inn, a village hall and an old forge. When The Street brings you to Station Hill, cross ahead into the churchyard and veer right, then over a stile in the far corner to enter Bourne Park.

It was in **Bishopsbourne** that novelist Joseph Conrad spent the last five years of his life. This tiny village was also home to writers Ford Madox Ford and Jocelyn Brooks.

The path cuts right through the parkland, crosses two footbridges and a stile in a dividing fence-line. When crossing the second section of parkland the stately red-brick Bourne House can be seen to the left. On the far side of the park a small lake is partly enclosed by trees; beyond it you come onto Bourne Park Road. A few paces after passing the fancy gateway to Bourne House take a footpath on the right, slanting uphill through the woodland of Warren Plantation. This brings you into a further section of Bourne Park where you bear left. A few oak posts direct the way across this parkland to the far bottom left-hand corner, where a stile takes you onto Bourne Park Road once more. A few more paces along this and you come to the main street in Bridge to complete the circuit.

Nearing the end of the walk, the way rises through Warren Plantation

WALK 38
Elham – Breach – Elham

Distance	7.5 miles/12km or 5.5 miles/9km
Map	OS Explorer 138 'Dover, Folkestone & Hythe' 1:25,000
Start	The Square, Elham (grid ref 177438)
Access	By bus from Canterbury and Folkestone
	Elham lies east of B2068, about 2 miles/3km northeast of Lyminge
Parking	In The Square near the parish church
Refreshments	Pubs and restaurant in Elham, tearoom in Breach

Exploring some of the best of Elham's attractive valley, this circuit has a mix of downland, woods and hilltop farmland, with fine views and lovely old buildings. Elham itself is graced by a number of charming buildings, and it would be worth spending time wandering the village streets to study some of them.

Note Although the main walk is not unduly strenuous, a shorter option is also described.

From the parish church in The Square walk down Duck Street to the Nailbourne stream, and enter the field on the left. Follow the Elham Valley Way to the far side of the field, turn right along the boundary, and shortly after cross a stile into the next field on the left. Keeping to its left-hand edge come to a narrow road at North Elham, turn right for a few paces, then left between houses. Go through a gate and walk slightly right ahead, then over a stile into a sloping strip of meadow below a modern house. Maintain direction along the hillside below Piercely Wood, guided by marker posts to a stile next to a field gate in the corner of a long meadow.

The **Elham Valley Way** runs for 22.5 miles/36km between Hythe and Canterbury, and was created by

Houses in The Square in Elham, where the walk begins

KCC in collaboration with two of the county's Countryside Management Projects – the Kentish Stour, and the White Cliffs Countryside Project. An illustrated guidebook to the walk has been produced by KCC (see Walk 43).

Over the stile keep to the lower edge of another meadow, but at the boundary corner where the path splits three ways, take the left-hand option, still signed for the Elham Valley Way and leading along the slope of Hall Downs. Reach a stile in the bottom corner of a meadow, and make for the left-hand side of Wingmore Court Farm. (**Note** The OS map shows the route going through the farmyard, but this is no longer the case.) Coming onto a road walk ahead for a few paces, then turn right on a lane leading past the farm. About 250m later cross a stile on the left next to a field gate. Turn

201

half-right and walk up the slope to a marker pole which indicates the way into Thomas Acre Wood, from whose edge there's a very pleasant view.

A fairly steep path climbs through the wood, then you emerge into a hilltop field and cross to a second field. Maintain direction, but note the view left into the valley stretching off to the village of Barham, whose church is clearly signalled by its green broach spire. At the far side of this field come to a junction of paths where the shorter option (Option B) leaves the main walk (Option A) at grid ref 195465.

OPTION A (MAIN WALK)

Turn left to follow the Elham Valley Way, which soon becomes a sunken track descending alongside woodland. On reaching a gate leave the EVW and bear right alongside a fence, soon reaching a track with Breach seen below, and Barham in the distance. Arriving at double farm gates, the right of way goes through the left-hand gate, and with Breach Farm ahead cuts across a sloping meadow to the right-hand of two bridle gates – this is different from that shown on the OS map. (**Note** Should you need refreshment, go to the lower gate, and on to the bottom left-hand corner of the meadow where another gate gives onto the road. Walk ahead for a short distance to find tearooms at the vineyard on the left.)

The main walk does not go through the bridle gate, but turns right to cross a section of the meadow to a kissing gate which gives onto the track you'd only recently left. Cross the track and go through a second kissing gate, then wander down into a little valley, through another kissing gate, across a farm drive and over a stile. Go up the slope to woodland lining the hill.

The path climbs steeply through the wood to a crossing track near the top of the slope. Turn right along this all the way to a narrow road beside a bungalow. Cross to a field and bear half-left to reach another narrow lane near some barns. Turn right for about 150m as far as a woodland shaw, then enter the field on the right and take the footpath which cuts back diagonally across it.

On the far side bear left to pass along the edge of a nursery to reach a large field. Aim half-right across it, then bear left at the far boundary. Shortly before it curves a little to the right, keep alert to follow a path running through the hedge to a stile giving access to the next large hilltop field. Bear half-right, and on the far side cross another stile onto a very narrow lane. Turn right. Within a few paces you will arrive at a junction of lanes to join the shorter walk at grid ref 195455.

The peaceful Elham Valley, near Breach

OPTION B (SHORTER WALK)

Turn right, and shortly after go along an enclosed track leading to another hilltop field. Maintain direction to a junction of lanes by Wingate Farm. Walk ahead along a narrow lane. At the next junction rejoin the main walk at grid ref 195455.

Both routes having combined at the road junction, head south and after a short distance where the lane curves by a cottage named Beam End, enter the field on the left where a footpath takes you towards a large grey barn seen ahead at Dreal's Farm. Through a gate pass to the left of a pond, then veer left to come onto yet another narrow lane by a flint-walled cottage. Turn right, and after about 70m a gate on the right gives access to a footpath cutting diagonally across another open field.

On the far side cross another narrow lane, go over a field corner to a second lane by a house named Sherwood, then over a stile leading into the next field. Walk ahead along the right-hand boundary until the fence breaks to the right. Now maintain direction across the brow of the hill to a field corner. Over another stile descend the right-hand edge of a sloping meadow. Elham can be seen in the valley below. Keep alongside the fence as it changes direction, then over a final stile continue down the slope through a large field. At the far side turn left for about 50m, then go through a gate on your right, cross the Nailbourne stream and branch left across a small meadow. A drive then takes you between houses to bring you to The Square near Elham church.

WALK 39
Sandwich – Sandwich Bay – Sandwich

Distance	6 miles/9.5km
Map	OS Explorer 150 'Canterbury & the Isle of Thanet' 1:25,000
Start	The Barbican, The Quay, Sandwich (grid ref 332583)
Access	By train between Minster and Deal
	By bus from Canterbury and Deal
	By road, Sandwich is reached by feeder roads off A256/A258
Parking	Several pay & display car parks within the town
Refreshments	Pubs, cafés and restaurants in Sandwich

From the heart of historic Sandwich to the open expanse of Sandwich Bay, this undemanding circular walk accompanies the River Stour, crosses low-lying grassland, and returns among a grid of waterways lively with heron, dragonfly and damselfly.

Starting by the Barbican on the south bank of the River Stour, head to the right beside the river along The Quay. Boats are usually drawn up here, while on the greensward there's a replica beacon which marks the 400th anniversary of the defeat of the Spanish Armada. On coming to an iron footbridge spanning a narrow tributary, cross and continue along a raised embankment. When the tarmac forks, take the left branch into open countryside. (The Saxon Shore Way, which has been followed from the start of the walk, now takes the right branch on a more direct route to Sandwich Bay. Our path, however, is shared by the Stour Valley Walk.)

The **Barbican gatehouse** was built in 1539 as part of a coastal defence system. Tolls were collected on the adjacent Stour bridge until 1977, and a board

The Barbican gate-house in Sandwich was built in 1539

showing the various charges is displayed within the Barbican's archway.

The path curves for a while alongside the Stour, then the tarmac finishes and you cross North Stream to a narrow road. After a few paces along this cross a stile on the right and wander through meadowland passing New Downs Farm on your left. About 200m beyond the farm the path veers half-left towards a large house seen some way ahead.

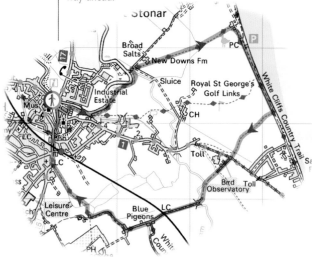

The Stour spills out at its estuary in **Pegwell Bay** where the Saxons under Hengist and Horsa landed in AD449. Almost 150 years later, in AD597, St Augustine made landfall there when bringing Christianity to Britain.

Come onto a track leading through Prince's Golf Links, with Sandwich Bay directly ahead. A short distance beyond the former clubhouse, turn right beside a fence on a footpath, with the sea now on your left. Walking parallel with Princes Drive go through a parking area and pass a toilet block. There's a second toilet block about 300m beyond the first, and within a few paces of this the route of the Saxon Shore Way joins ours once more. Keep ahead alongside Princes Drive for about 700m to find a stile on the right at grid ref 362579.

A tributary of the Stour on the outskirts of Sandwich

Crossing this stile you enter Royal St George's Golf Links, and leave the Saxon Shore Way once more. A path leads across the golf course, and when it forks on the far side, bear left, aiming towards Old Downs Farm. Cross a narrow lane, known as Guildford Road, onto a track leading past Sandwich Bay Bird Observatory, which houses a Field Study Centre.

A short distance beyond the Bird Observatory the track comes alongside a watercourse. When the track curves away, take a bridleway cutting ahead, then cross the watercourse on a concrete farm bridge. A hedge-lined track now strikes southwestward, crosses a railway line, and becomes a narrow paved lane by Blue Pigeons Farmhouse. When the lane curves sharply to the left by Temptye Farmhouse, take another lane on the right between low-lying farmland. This soon curves left alongside another watercourse and brings you to a solitary white house at grid ref 336567.

Turn right on a narrow tarmac footpath. At first flanked by reeds it crosses yet another watercourse and progresses through the middle of a large open field. Eventually come onto Deal Road and bear right, passing the former St Bartholomew's Hospital, and walk into Sandwich. Just beyond the railway station, note the old town wall – by following the broad raised footpath (Mill Wall) to the right you will come to The Quay and the Barbican where the walk began. Alternatively keep ahead, then branch right into Galliard Street which leads to the High Street, and thence to the Barbican.

A heron waits for a meal by a narrow watercourse

WALK 40
Dover (Langdon Cliffs) – St Margaret's at Cliffe – Langdon Cliffs

Distance	7 miles/11km
Map	OS Explorer 138 'Dover, Folkestone & Hythe' 1:25,000
Start	Langdon Cliffs Picnic Site (grid ref 335422)
Access	Northeast of Dover, reached via minor road (signed) branching east of the A258 about 1 mile/1.5km south of A2 roundabout (Jubilee Way)
Parking	Langdon Cliffs Picnic Site (NT owned – fee payable)
Refreshments	Coffee shop at Langdon Cliffs, pubs in St Margaret's at Cliffe

The White Cliffs of Dover have represented the gateway to England for centuries. Celebrated in literature, in song, on countless paintings and photographs, when seen from a homebound Channel ferry they symbolise much more than just an upthrusting wall of chalk. To the invading Romans they must have seemed impregnable. Above Dover the massive castle that overlooks both the town and the Channel itself was England's second line of defence after the White Cliffs, and not even Hitler's bombardment during the last war could raze it to the ground. Today it remains as stubbornly defiant as the cliffs on which it stands.

This walk has views of the castle, and of the cliffs. But it also explores a slightly tilted land of big fields with big skies stretched over all. It passes above St Margaret's Bay where tradition has it that Channel swimmers set out for France, and from the clifftop walk France itself can often be seen just 20 miles/32km away. Although the walk is described as starting from Langdon Cliffs, it could as easily begin in St Margaret's at Cliffe, served by bus from Dover and Deal. St Margaret's also has a free car park not far from the church, accessed via Reach Road.

Leaving the picnic site at its Dover-end entrance, walk down the twisting minor road to the bridge spanning the deep cut of the A2. Across the bridge with its fine view

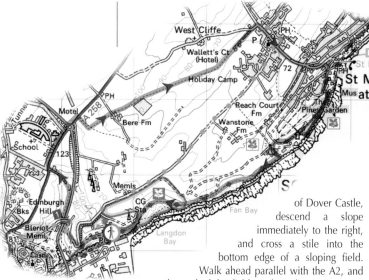

of Dover Castle, descend a slope immediately to the right, and cross a stile into the bottom edge of a sloping field. Walk ahead parallel with the A2, and at the end of the field go through a gate onto a stony farm track, and wander uphill to a pair of large barns. Pass between the barns, and just beyond them cross a stile onto a tarmac footpath beside the A258. Turn right and follow this to a roundabout on the busy A2.

Cross straight ahead with great care, and maintain direction along the continuing A258 for about 150m, where you will find a stile among trees on the right, immediately before the road curves. Over this walk along the left headland of a field. After another 150m cross a stile on the left, then go ahead between pillboxes along the right-hand edge of a field. Reaching its far corner cross another stile, then continue ahead over a farm track and alongside a flint-walled barn at Bere Farm. Beyond the farm buildings maintain direction on a footpath among trees, then emerge into a large field.

Keep along the right-hand boundary of the field to its far corner by Bere Wood, then pass through a gap into the field ahead. Veer slightly right across this very large open field. On the far side cross a stile and continue in the same direction to another stile. Over this you then follow the left fence-line to reach a track, formerly used to carry a railway during the last war. Passing more pillboxes the track brings you to a road leading to a T-junction where you bear right into St Margaret's at Cliffe.

St Margaret's at Cliffe has pubs, general stores and a post office. The church of St Margaret of Antioch has a massive, but stumpy Norman tower, and fine carvings round its west door. One of the stained glass windows is a memorial to those who died in the *Herald of Free Enterprise* disaster, when the ferry capsized off Zeebrugge in 1988. Three of the crew members who lost their lives came from St Margaret's.

Walk through the village and continue along the road as far as St Margaret's Bay where the road forks by a green. Turn right into St Margaret's Road, and after about 50m turn left down a tarmac drive. When it curves, go ahead down a flight of steps enclosed between a wall and a fence, then at the bottom turn right into Foreland Road. In another 100m fork left along The Crescent. On reaching a crossing track continue ahead, ignoring a footpath on the right. Rising among trees the track then curves right onto Lighthouse Down, but we go ahead through a kissing gate onto the clifftop, and turn right on the Saxon Shore Way. This is also part of a shorter walk known as the Frontline Britain Trail.

St Margaret's Bay is the closest part of the English coast to France, with Cap Blanc Nez just 20 miles/32km away. France can usually be seen quite clearly from the clifftop path. St Margaret's Bay was once a small fishing community, but it became notorious for a while as a haunt of smugglers. During World War II the famous guns, nicknamed Winnie and Pooh fired salvos across the Channel, and since 1972 a statue of Sir Winston Churchill has overlooked the bay, staring defiantly across the water.

The footpath leads along the top of the famous White Cliffs, but after a while it curves to the right to reach another kissing gate giving onto a chalk track. Bear left. Hidden among the trees nearby is St Margaret's Windmill, a smock mill built in 1928, but which ceased operating in 1939. There's also a disused lighthouse, barely seen from the track. Shortly before coming to a narrow road, leave the track and bear left towards the South Foreland Lighthouse at grid ref 359434.

South Foreland Lighthouse was built by Trinity House in 1843, and in 1858 was the first to be operated by electricity. In 1898 it was used by Marconi to demonstrate radio telegraphy. The lighthouse is now in the care of the National Trust, and is open Friday, Saturday, Sunday and Monday 11am–5pm end of April to October, and daily in school holidays (☎ 01304 852463). Accessed by 73 steps, the lighthouse balcony provides a splendid view across the Channel and over much of East Kent.

South Foreland Lighthouse is now owned by the National Trust

The clifftop path gives clear views of Dover Harbour

Take an enclosed footpath left of the lighthouse entrance gates, wander down to the clifftop and turn right along the route of the continuing Saxon Shore Way. With the chalk cliffs plunging into the surf to your left, as you progress along the grassland path, Dungeness Nuclear Power Station comes into view far away, while much nearer Dover Harbour is busy with the coming and going of cross-Channel ferries.

The path curves round the 'dry valley' of Fan Point, and soon after alternative trails are offered. Remain on the lower (cliff-side) path heading towards a large coastguard building. Cross a stile into the NT-owned Langdon Hole, and before long cross a brief grass track that once carried a railway line, then climb a flight of wood-braced steps. Follow a fence on your left, then through a gate wander across Langdon Cliffs with a direct view onto Dover Harbour, and come to the car park, picnic site and visitor centre.

The **Gateway to the White Cliffs Visitor Centre** on Langdon Cliffs has a number of information panels relating to the coast and nearby countryside, much of which forms part of the Heritage Coast and is a Site of Special Scientific Interest. The Visitor Centre also has a coffee shop, gift shop and public toilets. Guided walks are organised here by the National Trust throughout the year.

Langdon Cliffs (Walk 40)

LONGER WALKS

Kent has a number of long-distance walking routes. Some, like the North Downs Way and Greensand Way, journey right across the county, while others, such as the Elham Valley Way and Stour Valley Walk, explore specific features within the county's boundaries. Each one is worth tackling, either in its entirety, or as a basis for creating shorter day walks and circuits.

While Kent's only National Trail is the North Downs Way, others have been created by local groups of the Ramblers' Association, Kent County Council, District Councils, Borough Councils, or by the inspiration of individuals. Most link existing rights of way, sometimes by including a short stretch of green lane or country road where there are gaps between footpaths. Some LDPs may have no more than conventional finger posts or slim direction arrows as their waymark, but the majority have their own dedicated symbol to identify the continuing route. The Saxon Shore Way, for example, has a red Viking helmet; an acorn symbolises the North Downs Way; the head of a grey heron is the unique logo of the Stour Valley Walk.

Walking a long-distance route from start to finish is a rewarding experience, for there can be few better ways of discovering the true nature of the land through which the route journeys. Day by day you notice how the landscape unfolds to reveal its scenic diversity, and come to understand why villages and towns visited on the way are located where they are. Some routes follow a particular geographical feature, such as the River Medway or the long ridge of the Greensand Hills, while others – and the Wealdway is a prime example – strike across the county from one range of hills to another, from one valley system to the next, with all the changes of vegetation and land use that entails. Healthy exercise by day, and the pleasure that comes from meeting new people at each evening's B&B, all add to the experience, and at the end of a journey that has taken several days to complete you feel naturally uplifted by a sense of achievement.

Note The following list of long walks in Kent gives only the briefest of details, but anyone wishing to discover more about a specific route is advised to consult the recommended guidebook for further details.

WALK 41
The Darent Valley Path

Distance	19 miles/31km
Start	Sevenoaks
Finish	Dartford
Maps	OS Explorer 147 & 162 1:25,000
Guidebook	*Along and Around the Darent Valley Path* by Lorna Jenner & Eila Lawton (KCC)

Edmund Spencer's poem, *The Faerie Queen*, spoke of '...the silver Darent, in whose waters cleane/Ten thousand fishes play', and until fairly recent times that held good. Until, that is, industrial pollution in its lower reaches degraded this chalk stream that rises in the Greensand Hills south of Westerham, flows east through the Holmesdale Valley, then north through the Downs on its way to Dartford and the Thames. However, the river has since been greatly improved and carefully managed to bring it back to a semblance of its former glory, and the walk which joins the Darent near Chipstead on the outskirts of Sevenoaks soon delights in its abundant vegetation and wildlife. Between Shoreham and Lullingstone the river is lined with pollarded willows, and the footpath keeps close company with it (see Walk 1) before the Darent swings briefly behind Lullingstone Castle, on its journey to Eynsford. Between the Castle and Eynsford it's worth visiting Lullingstone Roman Villa, the most impressive of several Roman remains to be uncovered in the valley. Downstream from Farningham the footpath follows the Darent around the edge of Horton Kirby, goes alongside flooded gravel pits, and shortly after enters South Darenth. Busy Dartford is not far away, and although the countryside is lost by the time it enters the town, there's still interest to be drawn from this undemanding yet rewarding walk.

WALK 42
The Eden Valley Walk

Distance	15 miles/24km
Start	Edenbridge
Finish	Tonbridge
Map	OS Explorer 147 1:25,000
Guidebook	*Eden Valley Walk* by Caroline Wing (KCC)

An early tributary of the Medway, the River Eden enters Kent from Surrey among low-lying meadows on the outskirts of Edenbridge. The Eden Valley Walk follows the course of this river, where possible, as far as Penshurst where it joins the Medway, then continues all the way to Tonbridge beside that broader river. Five miles out of Edenbridge the route passes through Hever, a tiny village whose lovely old castle was the childhood home of Anne Boleyn, second wife of Henry VIII and mother of the first Queen Elizabeth. Not long after leaving Hever the way skirts Chiddingstone, a one-street village with a 600-year history (see Walk 13), then goes through meadows and woods on the way to Penshurst, another fine village noted for the impressive Penshurst Place which dates from at least the 13th century (see Walks 14 and 15). The Eden and Medway come together in meadows below the village, while the EVW strikes through parkland to rejoin the waterway south of Leigh, then keeps company with it all the way into Tonbridge. By combining the Eden Valley Walk with the Medway Valley Walk (see below), it's possible to make a continuous journey by footpath and short stretches of road walking right across Kent.

WALK 43
The Elham Valley Way

Distance	22.5 miles/36km
Start	Hythe
Finish	Canterbury
Maps	OS Explorer 138 & 150 1:25,000
Guidebook	*Along and Around the Elham Valley Way* by Brian Hart & Eila Lawton (KCC)

This splendid recreational route explores the unspoilt Elham Valley which lies below the North Downs in East Kent. It visits a string of lovely villages, follows the intermittent Nailbourne stream, and occasionally edges along the downland slope to gain striking panoramic views. Two walks in this present collection are based on that longer route, giving some of the best walking and nicest views of the valley. See Walks 37 and 38.

WALK 44
The Greensand Way

Distance	110 miles/177km
Start	Haslemere (Surrey)
Finish	Hamstreet
Maps	OS Explorer 125, 133, 136, 137, 145, 146, 147 & 148 1:25,000
Guidebook	*Along and Around the Greensand Way* by Bea Cowan (KCC)

As its name implies, the Greensand Way follows the line of the Greensand Hills across Surrey and Kent, through some of the finest countryside in all southern England.

Entering Kent in woodland at Crockham Hill the route, waymarked with an oasthouse logo, heads eastward along the ridge to Toys Hill, Ide Hill and Knole Park in Sevenoaks. Beyond Ightham Mote the GW deserts the ridge to visit Shipbourne, then regains higher ground before descending to cross the Medway at Yalding. After this it's orchard country for a while, with extensive views from the ridge crest; then among parkland and tiny hamlets as the way curves towards the south, to Egerton and Pluckley. Bypassing Hothfield, the route visits Great Chart near Ashford, and continues to Kingsnorth before completing its journey at Hamstreet, on the route of the Saxon Shore Way. Several walks in this book adopt sections of the Greensand Way.

WALK 45
The High Weald Walk

Distance	28 miles/45km
Start/Finish	Bullingstone/Speldhurst
Maps	OS Explorer 135, 136 & 147 1:25,000
Guidebook	*Along and Around the High Weald Walk* by Bea Cowan (KCC)

Making a circular tour through the High Weald AONB around Tunbridge Wells, this recreational route was developed by a partnership between KCC, Tunbridge Wells Borough Council and the Countryside Commission. It's an area of abrupt hills and fertile vales, and the walk weaves a course through some of the best by way of linking footpaths and hedge-lined lanes. South of Tunbridge Wells the High Weald Walk strays into East Sussex, but the majority of the route lies within Kent. Being a circular walk it could begin, of course, at one of many different places. The guidebook is written with a start in the hamlet of Bullingstone near Speldhurst.

WALK 46
The Medway Valley Walk

Distance	28 miles/45km
Start	Tonbridge
Finish	Rochester
Maps	OS Explorer 147 & 148 1:25,000
Guidebook	*Medway Valley Walk* by Kev Reynolds (KCC)

Tracing the Medway navigation downstream to its estuary at Rochester, this route takes the walker through the heart of the county. From Tonbridge to Aylesford the walk keeps almost entirely to the towpath, but is forced away from the river bank for a short distance before returning to it for the final approach to Rochester, overlooked by the gaunt Norman castle. The walk actually begins beneath the walls of Tonbridge Castle, another Norman edifice whose drum towers are best seen across neat lawns and flowerbeds. Turning your back on Tonbridge the walk is drawn through the river's peaceful corridor, only rarely passing through villages or towns. It's a colourful route with the added interest of river craft negotiating the many lock gates that control much of the Medway. Within this present collection of routes, Walk 19 samples a section of the Medway Valley Walk in its circuit from Teston Bridge.

On the route of the Medway Valley Walk near Rochester

WALK 47
The North Downs Way

Distance	123 miles/198km or 130 miles/208km via Canterbury
Start	Farnham (Surrey)
Finish	Dover
Maps	OS Explorer 137, 138, 145, 146, 147, 148, 149 & 150 1:25,000
Guidebook	*The North Downs Way* by Kev Reynolds (Cicerone)
	North Downs Way by Neil Curtis (Aurum Press)

The North Downs Way National Trail was officially opened in September 1978, and soon established a reputation as one of the premier long-distance walks of southern England. Like the Greensand Way it begins in Surrey, but enters Kent above Westerham, crosses the Darent Gap at Otford, and climbs onto the Downs once more above Kemsing. A long woodland section takes the route towards the Medway, which is crossed on a bridge beside the M2 outside Rochester. Then, arcing towards the southeast, peace is regained on the way to Wye, where the Downs have again been cut by a river; this time it's the Stour. The NDW forks shortly before reaching the river. One branch heads away to visit Canterbury before crossing a big open land on the way to Dover, while the more direct route regains the crest of the Downs above Wye on one of the most rewarding of all stages. This leads eventually to Etchinghill, and on to Shakespeare Cliff overlooking Dover.

WALK 48
The Royal Military Canal Path

Distance	28 miles/45km
Start	Seabrook near Hythe
Finish	Cliff End near Rye (Sussex)
Map	OS Explorer 125 & 138 1:25,000
Guidebook	*Royal Military Canal* (a pack containing 10 self-guided circular walks)

Built between 1804 and 1809 as part of the British defence system against feared invasion by Napoleon, the Royal Military Canal forms the inland boundary of Romney Marsh. It was created in two sections: the longest running from Hythe to Iden Lock in East Sussex; the other, much shorter, section going from below Winchelsea Hill to Cliff End. With the fall of Napoleon, the Canal lost its military purpose, and a civilian barge service was then established between Hythe and Rye which lasted until the mid-19th century. Today the Canal is used as a means of managing water levels on the Romney and Walland Marshes, while the towpath offers peaceful walking opportunities. Sheep graze the banks; dragonflies, damselflies and kingfishers may be seen, while springtime is noisy with the croaking of Marsh frogs. Walk 24 traces a section of the Canal path, but for more information visit the Romney Marsh Countryside Project website: **www.royalmilitarycanal.com**

The Royal Military Canal Path

WALK 49
The Saxon Shore Way

Distance	163 miles/262km
Start	Gravesend
Finish	Hastings (Sussex)
Maps	OS Explorer 124, 125, 138, 148, 149, 150 & 163 1:25,000
Guidebook	*The Saxon Shore Way* by Bea Cowan (Aurum Press)

Sign for the Saxon Shore Way on the edge of Romney Marsh

Both a long-distance walk and a trail through history, the Saxon Shore Way traces as far as possible the coastline as it was in Saxon times, on the way passing numerous sites of historic interest. The shoreline is of considerable interest to naturalists, especially along the Swale where birdlife is plentiful. But as the coastline has changed dramatically over the years, the SSW often strays inland, especially round the edge of Thanet and on the landward

side of Romney Marsh, before crossing the county boundary on the approach to Rye in Sussex. The trail offers a surprising diversity of scenery, from the marshlands of the Thames and Medway estuaries to the White Cliffs of Dover, and from the low-lying farmland of Thanet to memorable vantage points on the escarpment of an ancient coastline between Folkestone and Appledore. The Swale Heritage Trail gives circular walks based on sections of the Saxon Shore Way, and several other walks in this book adopt parts of the SSW route.

WALK 50
The Stour Valley Walk

Distance	51 miles/82km
Start	Lenham
Finish	Shell Ness, Pegwell Bay
Maps	OS Explorer 137 & 150 1:25,000
Guidebook	*Stour Valley Walk* by Veronica Litten (KCC)

Following the Great Stour from its source to the sea, this is a delightful walk, full of interest and variety. At first a modest stream that meanders through both parkland and farmland, it grows in importance on its way towards Ashford. On the approach to Canterbury the river divides, then reforms before flowing through Fordwich, the medieval port of Canterbury. One of the most interesting sections of the walk traces the course of the river among the tall reedbeds of Stodmarsh Nature Reserve (see Walk 35) leading to Grove Ferry. Beyond this the Stour is tidal, and the sea beckons, but the river makes a long sweep southeast to Sandwich, after which the SVW deserts the Stour by heading for Sandwich Bay, and only rejoining it as the river spills into the sea at the Shell Ness headland overlooking Pegwell Bay.

WALK 51
The Wealdway

Distance	82 miles/132km
Start	Gravesend
Finish	Beachy Head/Eastbourne (Sussex)
Maps	OS Explorer 123, 135, 147, 148 & 163 1:25,000
Guidebook	*The Wealdway & The Vanguard Way* by Kev Reynolds (Cicerone)
	Along and Around the Wealdway by Helen Livingston (KCC)

Near Luddesdown the Wealdway passes through an area known as the Bowling Alley

From the River Thames to the English Channel, the Wealdway strikes across the North Downs and Greensand Ridge, follows the Medway into Tonbridge, then climbs over a High Weald ridge before entering Sussex near Ashurst. The Sussex half of the walk is also very fine, with the crossing of Ashdown Forest being a highlight, and the South Downs making a memorable finalé. The Wealdway explores some of the most deserted countryside in the southeast, and deserves to be better known.

APPENDIX I
ROUTE TABLE

West Kent and The Weald

Walk	Distance	Maps	Start
1 Lullingstone Park – Shoreham – Lullingstone Park	6.5 miles/10.5km	OS Explorer 147 & 162 1:25,000	Lullingstone Park Visitor Centre
2 Shoreham – Romney Street – Shoreham	5 miles/8km	OS Explorer 147 1:25,000	Church of St Peter & St Paul, Shoreham
3 Westerham – French Street – Chartwell – Westerham	5 miles/8km	OS Explorer 147 1:25,000	Westerham green
4 Crockham Hill – Toys Hill – Obriss – Crockham Hill	5 miles/8km	OS Explorer 147 1:25,000	Church Road, Crockham Hill

Walk	Distance	Maps	Start
5 Toys Hill – Ide Hill – Crockham Hill – French Street – Toys Hill	9 miles/14.5km	OS Explorer 147 1:25,000	National Trust car park, Toys Hill
6 Ide Hill – Manor Farm – Ide Hill	5 miles/8km	OS Explorer 147 1:25,000	Ide Hill village green
7 Sevenoaks Weald – Boarhill – Sevenoaks Weald	6 miles/9.5km	OS Explorer 147 1:25,000	St George's church, Sevenoaks Weald
8 Shipbourne – Underriver – Ightham Mote – Shipbourne	6.5 miles/10.5km	OS Explorer 147 1:25,000	Shipbourne church
9 Four Elms – Winkhurst Green – Bough Beech – Four Elms	7 miles/11km	OS Explorer 147 1:25,000	The Four Elms pub, Four Elms
10 Marsh Green – Crippenden Manor – Marsh Green	5.5 miles/9km	OS Explorer 147 1:25,000	The village green, Marsh Green
11 Cowden – Horseshoe Green – Bassett's Farm – Cowden	6 miles/10km	OS Explorer 147 1:25,000	By Cowden church
12 Cowden – Hoath Corner – Cowden	8.5 miles/13.5km	OS Explorer 147 1:25,000	By Cowden church

No. & Route	Distance	Map	Start
13 Chiddingstone – Penshurst – Chiddingstone	6.5 miles/10.5km	OS Explorer 147 1:25,000	St Mary's church, Chiddingstone
14 Penshurst – Salmans – Nashes Farm – Penshurst	5.5 miles/9km	OS Explorer 147 1:25,000	Opposite Penshurst Place on B2176
15 Penshurst – Fordcombe – Penshurst	7 miles/11km	OS Explorer 147 1:25,000	Leicester Square, Penshurst
16 Groombridge – Speldhurst – Groombridge	7 miles/11km	OS Explorer 135 & 147 1:25,000	The Crown Inn, Groombridge
17 Brenchley – Matfield – Brenchley	7 miles/11km	OS Explorer 136 1:25,000	Brenchley church
18 Yalding – Hunton – Buston Manor – Yalding	6.5 miles/10.5km	OS Explorer 136 & 148 1:25,000	Yalding church
19 Teston Bridge – Wateringbury – Kettle Corner – Teston Bridge	5.5 miles/9km	OS Explorer 148 1:25,000	Teston Bridge Picnic Site, Teston
20 Linton – Boughton Monchelsea Place – Linton	5 miles/8km	OS Explorer 136 & 148 1:25,000	Linton church
21 Ulcombe Church – Boughton Malherbe – Grafty Green – Ulcombe	7.5 miles/12km	OS Explorer 137 1:25,000	Ulcombe church

Walk	Distance	Maps	Start
22 Pluckley – Little Chart – Egerton – Pluckley	6.5 miles/10.5km	OS Explorer 137 1:25,000	Pluckley playing field
23 Tenterden (Wittersham Road) – Small Hythe – Tenterden	5.5 miles/9km	OS Explorer 125 1:25,000	Wittersham Road Railway Station (K&ES Railway)
24 Appledore – Stone-in-Oxney – Royal Military Canal – Appledore	7.5 miles/12km	OS Explorer 125 1:25,000	Court Lodge Road, Appledore

North and East Kent

Walk	Distance	Maps	Start
25 Camer Country Park – Luddesdown – Great Buckland – Camer Country Park	6 miles/9.5km	OS Explorer 148 1:25,000	Camer Country Park, Meopham
26 Stansted – Fairseat – Hodsoll Street – Ridley – Stansted	5.5 miles/9km	OS Explorer 148 1:25,000	The Black Horse, Stansted
27 Trosley Country Park – Coldrum Stones – Ryarsh – Trosley Country Park	6.5 miles/10.5km	OS Explorer 148 1:25,000	Trosley Country Park
28 Newington – Upchurch – Lower Halstow – Newington	7 miles/11km	OS Explorer 148 1:25,000	Newington High Street

29 Leysdown-on-Sea – Shellness – Harty – Leysdown-on-Sea	7 miles/11km	OS Explorer 149 1:25,000	Leysdown Country & Coastal Park
30 Faversham – Oare Creek – Uplees – Oare – Faversham	6.5 miles/10.5km	OS Explorer 149 1:25,000	The Guildhall, Faversham Market Place
31 Faversham – Ham Marshes – Oare Creek – Faversham	5 miles/8km	OS Explorer 149 1:25,000	The Guildhall, Faversham Market Place
32 Wye – Crundale – Coombe Manor – Wye	7 miles/11km	OS Explorer 137 1:25,000	Wye church
33 Wye – Wye Downs – Cold Blow – Wye	5.5 miles/9km	OS Explorer 137 1:25,000	Wye church
34 Chilham – Julliberrie Downs – Chilham	5 miles/8km	OS Explorer 137 1:25,000	The Square, Chilham
35 Stodmarsh Nature Reserve – Grove Ferry – Stodmarsh	4.5 miles/7km	OS Explorer 150 1:25,000	Stodmarsh National Nature Reserve car park
36 St Nicholas at Wade – Chitty – Sarre – St Nicholas at Wade	6.5 miles/10.5km	OS Explorer 150 1:25,000	St Nicholas church, St Nicholas at Wade
37 Bridge – Patrixbourne – Kingston – Bishopsbourne – Bridge	6.5 miles/10.5km	OS Explorer 150 1:25,000	Bridge High Street

Walk	Distance	Maps	Start	Finish
38 Elham – Breach – Elham	7.5 miles/12km or 5.5 miles/9km	OS Explorer 138 1:25,000	The Square, Elham	
39 Sandwich – Sandwich Bay – Sandwich	6 miles/9.5km	OS Explorer 150 1:25,000	The Barbican, The Quay, Sandwich	
40 Dover (Langdon Cliffs) – St Margaret's at Cliffe – Langdon Cliffs	7 miles/11km	OS Explorer 138 1:25,000	Langdon Cliffs Picnic Site	

Longer Walks

Walk	Distance	Maps	Start	Finish
41 The Darent Valley Path	19 miles/31km	OS Explorer 147 & 162 1:25,000	Sevenoaks	Dartford
42 The Eden Valley Walk	15 miles/24km	OS Explorer 147 1:25,000	Edenbridge	Tonbridge
43 The Elham Valley Way	22.5 miles/36km	OS Explorer 138 & 150 1:25,000	Hythe	Canterbury

44 The Greensand Way	110 miles/177km	OS Explorer 125133, 136, 137, 145, 146, 147 & 148 1:25,000	Haslemere (Surrey)	Hamstreet ,
45 The High Weald Walk	28 miles/45km	OS Explorer 135, 136 & 147 1:25,000	Bullingstone	Speldhurst
46 The Medway Valley Walk	28 miles/45km	OS Explorer 147 & 148 1:25,000	Tonbridge	Rochester
47 North Downs Way	123 miles/198km or 130 miles/208km via Canterbury	OS Explorer 137, 138, 145, 146, 147, 148, 149 & 150 1:25,000	Farnham (Surrey)	Dover
48 The Royal Military Canal Path	28 miles/45km	OS Explorer 125 & 138 1:25,000	Seabrook near Hythe	Cliff End near Rye (Sussex)
49 The Saxon Shore Way	163 miles/262km	OS Explorer 124, 125, 138, 148, 149, 150 & 163 1:25,000	Gravesend	Hastings (Sussex)
50 The Stour Valley Walk	51 miles/82km	OS Explorer 137 & 150 1:25,000	Lenham	Shell Ness, Pegwell Bay
51 The Wealdway	82 miles/132km	OS Explorer 123, 135, 147, 148 & 163 1:25,000	Gravesend	Beachy Head/ Eastbourne (Sussex)

APPENDIX II
USEFUL ADDRESSES

1 Campaign to Protect Rural England (CPRE)
☎ 020 7981 2800
www.cpre.org.uk

2 English Heritage
☎ 0870 333 1181
www.english-heritage.org.uk/southeast

3 Kent County Council
County Hall
Maidstone ME14 1XQ
☎ 01622 671411
www.kent.gov.uk
www.kent.gov.uk/countrysideaccess

4 Kent Wildlife Trust
Tyland Barn
Sandling
Maidstone ME14 3BD
☎ 01622 662012

5 The National Trust
PO Box 39
Warrington WA5 7WD
☎ 0870 458 4000
www.thenationaltrust.org.uk

6 The Ramblers' Association
2nd Floor, Camelford House
87-90 Albert Embankment
London SE1 7TW
☎ 020 7339 8500
www.ramblers.org.uk

APPENDIX III
RECOMMENDED READING

Illustrated Guide to Britain (AA/Drive Publications, 1974)

Belloc, Hilaire *The Old Road* (Constable, 1904)

Bignall, Alan *Kent Lore* (Robert Hale, 1983)

    The Kent Village Book (Countryside Books, 1986)

Burnham, Paul & McRae, Stuart *Kent: The Garden of England* (Paul Norbury Publications)

Church, Richard *Kent* (Robert Hale, 1948)

Cobbett, William *Rural Rides* (1912 edition)

Davis, P. *Leisure Guides – Kent* (Robert Hale, 1989)

Hughes, Pennethorne *Kent – A Shell Guide* (Faber & Faber)

Kaye-Smith, Sheila *Weald of Kent and Sussex* (Robert Hale, 1953)

Mason, Oliver *South-East England* (Bartholomew, 1979)

Maxwell, D. *Unknown Kent* (Bodley Head, 1921)

McNay, M. *Red Guide – Kent* (Waymark Publications/AA, 1989)

Mee, Arthur *The King's England – Kent* (Hodder & Stoughton, 1969)

Newman, John *North-East & East Kent* and *West Kent & The Weald* – The Buildings of England series (ed) Pevsner, N. (Penguin, 1976)

Nicolson, Nigel *Kent* (Wiedenfeld & Nicolson)

Rackham, Oliver *The History of the Countryside* (Wiedenfeld & Nicolson)

Reynolds, Kev *Classic Walks in Southern England* (Oxford Illustrated Press, 1990)

    The Visitor's Guide to Kent (Moorland Publishing, 1990)

Sankey, John *Nature Guide to South-East England* (Usborne, 1981)

Seymour, John *The Countryside Explained* (Penguin, 1979)

Spence, Keith *The Companion Guide to Kent & Sussex* (Collins, 1973)

Vigar, John *Exploring Kent Churches* (Meresborough, 1985)

Vine, P. *The Royal Military Canal* (David & Charles)

Webb, W. *Kent's Historic Buildings* (Robert Hale)